Woman's Day®

DECORATING WITH FABRIC

Sedgewood® Press

New York

For Diamandis Communications Inc.

Editorial Project Director: *Geraldine Rhoads*
Writer: *Elaine Green*
Instructions: *Helen Donnally*
Administrative Assistant: *Grace Westing*

For Sedgewood® Press

Director: *Elizabeth P. Rice*
Editorial Project Manager: *Connie Schrader*
Project Editor: *Amy Handy*
Production Manager: *Bill Rose*
Distributed by Meredith Corporation,
Des Moines, Iowa.

ISBN 0-696-02330-X
Library of Congress Catalog Card Number:
88-062570
Printed in the United States of America
10   9   8   7   6   5   4   3   2   1

ACKNOWLEDGMENTS

Two editors of *Woman's Day* produced virtually all of the stories in this book: Pamela Abrahams, Home Design Editor, and Theresa Capuana, Needlework and Creative Crafts Editor.

They are responsible for the eclectic decorating tastes that pervade the book. They perceived the pride that today's busy but creative home decorator may take from showing off her skills at the sewing machine, but also the pleasure she feels at achieving a quick fix for a drab room—so they guided both their freelance and their gifted staff designers in the development of projects suiting both needs.

So 18 projects offer the time-saving benefits of working with sheets. These include Bringing in the Sunshine, 20; From Sheets to Country Chic, 32; Family Album Screen, 56; Delicious Victoriana, 100; Is There a Princess in the House?, 110; Botanical Bedroom, 128; and Territorial Gain, 140, produced with assistance from J.P. Stevens.

Another eight features represent creative ways to achieve special effects with ready-made draperies and curtains. These stories, using readymades from Burlington Industries, are A Feeling of Movement, 28; Readymades Dress Tricky Windows, 40; Flaunt a Special Feature, 44; Poufs in Their Place, 68; Customizing Ready-Made Shades, 78; Priscilla Power, 123; Four-Way Window Treatment, 137.

Hanky-Panky, the bedroom deriving its charm from accessories fashioned from dyed handkerchiefs, was done with technical advice from Rit.

The Photographers:

Peter Billard: Lace Butterfly at the Window, 108; A Quilt Can Warm More Than a Bed, 138.

Peter Bosch: The Return of the Lace Curtain, 46.

Jon Elliott: Checkmates, 82.

Susan Gilmore: Flaunt a Special Feature, 44.

Mark Hofmann: Readymades Dress Tricky Windows, 40.

James Levin: Bringing in the Sunshine, 20; From Sheets to Country Chic, 32; The Pride of the Pantry, 87; Hard-Working Sink Skirt, 97; Is There a Princess in the House?, 110; Inside Shutters for Longer Nights, 150; Cozying Up with One Fabric, 156.

Keith Scott Morton: The Warmth of Country French, 14; Practical and Pretty, 50; Family Album Screen, 56; Chintz-Lined Bower, 74; Ruffles in View, 86; Dingy Bathroom Soaks Up Color, 90; Glorious Gallicism, 114; Botanical Bedroom, 128; Cozy Cocoon of Flannel Sheets, 132; Territorial Gain, 140; Starting Young in the Decorating Game, 144.

Geoffrey Nilsen: A Feeling of Movement, 28.

Designers

CONTENTS

ACCENTS

STAGE SETS FOR ENTERTAINING

THE KITCHEN AS PEOPLE-CENTER

PRETTY AIRS FOR THE BATH

THE BEDROOM AS MOOD-MAKER

SETTINGS FOR THE YOUNG SET

Dear Decorator:

Most Americans regard their homes as extensions of themselves. From the Pilgrims' small dwellings to today's houses, cottages, mansions and apartments, American homes provide a welcome haven for family and visitors. We hope that *Woman's Day*® DECORATING WITH FABRIC will help you make your home reflect your taste and style.

This book combines the efforts of many people. The editors of *Woman's Day* have been leaders in presenting the best in practical methods for home decorating to their readers, and they saw a need to bring together many of their best, most workable ideas in one volume. When we at Sedgewood were presented with the project, we were delighted.

As writers and editors worked to select and organize the materials, each became especially enthusiastic about certain projects. Many of us wanted to re-create *Delicious Victoriana*. (If you turn to page 100, I think you'll see why it became a favorite.) We hope you'll discover several projects that you really want to try and that will prove to be your favorites.

At Sedgewood® Press, we are dedicated to bringing you quality books with fine designs, traditional and unusual uses for projects, clear instructions, and lots of color. We hope you will enjoy *Woman's Day* DECORATING WITH FABRIC, and will look forward to more craft books from Sedgewood® Press.

Sincerely yours,

Connie Schrader

Connie Schrader
Editorial Project Manager

INTRODUCTION

Although few of us can make beautiful wood furniture, or weave carpets, or construct comfortable upholstered pieces we *can* work wonders in decorating with a component that is vital to every room's success: fabric. With a knowledge of basic straight-seam sewing and often with only the ability to cut, staple and glue material, an amateur can create style, mood, and livability in any room or space.

Think of a bedroom with and without full, long curtains—the difference between the pictures is coziness and a sense of luxury. Think of a living room with upholstered furniture that has seen better days. Then picture the same room with fresh slipcovers and curtains in a crisp yet romantic French country cotton. The difference is between drab and dramatic, and it is all done with fabric.

Your miracles can be little ones, too. What about paintbox-color cloth shutters for your child's room? Wake-me-up shower curtains and window treatment for a dreary bathroom? Sunny kitchen curtains out of checkered bistro tablecloth material?

Which room in your house is the least inviting? Confront it, look at it with new eyes and invent a fabric solution. There surely is one, and you may well find it among the scores of ideas in this book.

THE COMPANIONABLE LIVING ROOM

The most welcoming living rooms are not the formal set pieces some of us think we should have but relaxed, personal places that reflect our families, our interests, our tastes and talents. The homemade and the handmade produce the warmth our guests respond to.

THE WARMTH OF COUNTRY FRENCH

**D**raperies, table skirts, pillows, and screens in those characteristically bright and endearing French florals and paisleys help you create a farmhouse look with a special Gallic flavor.

Fabrics
Fabrics are 54-inch-wide cotton in coordinated prints.
Fabric A: Off-white print
Fabric B: Off-white striped print
Fabric C: Striped cinnamon print
Fabric D: Off-white print
Fabric E: Off-white print

One width each of prints B and C should have a repeat of stripes about 6¾ inches wide, to be used as border appliqués on the other fabrics.

Pinch-pleated Draperies

MATERIALS
Fabric A, see instructions to estimate yardage
Border fabric B, length of one drapery panel
Lining, same yardage as fabric A
Pleater tape, triple-pleat, and hooks enough for two drapery panels
Wooden drapery pole
Wooden curtain rings
Cup hooks, 2
Curtain rings, 2 small, metal

To determine yardage of fabric A, measure from top of window to floor, then add 4 inches for hems. For width, follow the chart that comes with the pleater tape.

From fabric A and lining, cut panels, adding 1-inch seam allowance at each side. From fabric B, cut two strips the length of the drapery panels. Press the sides under ½ inch, then topstitch the border strips ½ inch in from the edge of the panel.

Line draperies by stitching fabric panel A and lining panel together, right sides facing, along top and side edges. Turn them right side out and press.

Stitch pleater tape to the top of the panel as directed on the package. Hem panel A and lining separately. Insert the pleater hooks in the tape and hang on wooden rings.

For tiebacks, cut two B strips and two lining strips each about 20 inches long. With right sides together, stitch a B strip to a lining strip, leaving 3 inches open for turning. Turn the tiebacks right side out and sew the opening closed. Fold in half crosswise and sew a snap to top pair of matching corners; sew a small metal ring to one of those corners.

Screw a cup hook into the window frame; wrap a tieback around each drapery panel; snap fasteners closed and slip the rings over the cup hooks.

Pillows

Note: Instructions in brackets are for large pillows.

MATERIALS
Fabric A [D], ¾ yard [2 yards] for back and front

Border fabric B, ¾ yard [1 yard]
Pillow form, 18 inches [30 inches], boxed-edged and muslin-covered

Cut two 21-inch [35-inch] squares of fabric A [D] for back and front. Mark 18 inches [30 inches] square centered on front piece. Cut four 5½ × 20-inch [6½ × 32-inch] C strips, press sides under ½ inch and pin within the marked square, mitering the corners (see General Directions); topstitch the edges.

With right sides facing, leaving 18 inches open at center of one side, stitch back and front together. Spread the corners so the adjacent seams match; stitch across the corners 2 inches [4 inches] from points. Turn the cover right side out, insert the pillow form, and sew closed.

Folding Screen

MATERIALS
Three plywood panels, each
    20 × 72 × ½-inch-thick
Fabric E, 4 yards to cover one side of
    each panel
Fabric C, 2 yards for borders
Felt, 4 yards, 45 inches wide for backing
Thin quilt batts, three 20 × 72-inch
    panels for padding
White glue
Staple gun
Hinges, 4

Staple a quilt batt panel to one side of each plywood panel. Cut three

24 × 76-inch pieces of fabric E. Lay them facedown on the floor; center a panel, batting side down, over each. Stretching the fabric over panel edges, staple it to the back, starting at center of each side and working to corners.

From C, cut two 8½-inch-wide × 76-inch-long side borders. Topstitch ½-inch hem on inner edge of each. Wrapping excess to the back, glue one border to each of two panels. Cut top and bottom borders for all the panels; hem inner edges. Miter the corners (see General Directions) and glue the borders in place.

Cut three 20 × 72-inch felt panels and glue them to the backs of the panels. Attach hinges, screwing them through the fabric.

Tablecloth

MATERIALS
Fabric A, 1¼ yards for top cloth
Fabric C, 1½ yards for border
Fabric D, twice the floor-over-table-to-floor measurement for under-cloth

For top cloth cut a 43-inch square of fabric A. Turn edges ½ inch to right side; topstitch. Cut four 6½-inch-wide strips of fabric C to fit around the cloth; topstitch to cloth, folding edges under and mitering the corners (see General Directions).

For under-cloth measure from the floor, over the table, and to the floor. Adding 1 inch for hem, cut a circle (see General Directions) or a square from fabric D, piecing as necessary, then hem the edge.

DELIGHTFULLY OFF BALANCE

A swagged curtain forming a jabot on one side and fanning out on the floor on the other has a lot of dash. Two brass door pulls that hold the loosely knotted length of cloth look like authentic antique tieback rosettes.

MATERIALS

Fabric, lightweight (see instructions and General Directions to estimate yardage with string)
Brass door pulls, 2
Staple gun

Fasten the door pulls to the upper corners of the window frame. Drape the fabric over the pulls, then loosely knot it around each pull, stretching the top edge of the fabric straight across the window frame. Staple the top edge over the edge of the frame to anchor the fabric.

BRINGING IN THE SUNSHINE

**A** dismal "sun room" will finally live up to its name with a triple-skirted love seat, exuberant fringed balloon shades, and double-draped table. Wield your pinking shears and avoid a lot of hemming.

Balloon Shades

MATERIALS

Fabrics or sheets, 1 floral print and 2 solid colors for shade (see Balloon Shades under General Directions to estimate yardage; see instructions to estimate yardage for ruffling)

Shirring tape, the width of shade

Roman shade ring tape, the length of shade for each balloon, plus 1 more length

Pull-cord, 8 times the length of shade

Wooden strip, 1 inch × 2 inches × the width of window frame, for mounting board

Screw eyes, 1 for each vertical channel between balloons and 1 for each side edge (the opening must be large enough to accommodate all cords easily—see instructions)

Pinking shears

Angle irons, 2

Staple gun, with ½-inch staples

Cleat or ring, to fasten pull-cords

Thin metal rod, width of finished shade

Yardstick

To make shade, see Balloon Shades under General Directions, adding ruffling as follows.

You will need three tiers of ruffling, one floral and one of each solid color. Cut each ruffle strip 2½ times as long as

the width of the shade, piecing as necessary and cutting the floral strip 2½ inches wide, one solid-color strip 3¼ inches wide, and the other solid-color strip 4 inches wide. Pink one edge of each strip. Hem the ends.

Stack the tiers with the narrowest on top, then pin them together with the straight edges matching. Gather the tiers to the width of the shade. With right sides matching, and allowing ½-inch stitch for seam, stitch the ruffle to the lower edge of shade. Complete shade as specified under General Directions.

Settee Cover

MATERIALS
Fabrics or sheets to match shade (see instructions to estimate yardages)
Foam seat cushion, 4 to 6 inches thick, muslin-covered (or cover original cushion)
2-string shirring tape, 2½ times measurement around settee cushion

For the cushion you will need one piece of fabric to cover the top and sides of the cushion and one piece to cover the bottom, adding ½-inch seam allowance to all edges. Cut out the two pieces.

Place the top piece, wrong side up, on the cushion and pin the corners to fit. Stitch corners and trim away excess.

With right sides together, stitch the top and bottom together, leaving the back open. Turn right side out, then insert the cushion and baste the opening closed.

For the flounce, you will need a three-tiered ruffle as for the Balloon Shades, cutting each tier 2½ times the measurement around the cushion. Cut the widest solid-color tier 2 inches wider than seat-to-floor measurement, the center solid-color tier 3 inches narrower, and the top floral tier 6 inches narrower. Hem, pink, and pin as for the shade. Turn the straight edge under 2 inches and baste. Stitch the shirring tape on the wrong side 1 inch below the top edge. Pull the strings, gathering the flounce to fit. Tack around the settee.

Pillows

MATERIALS
Fabrics (or sheets), to match shades;
    1¼ yards 45-inch-wide floral for
    2 pillows with tiered ruffle
¾ yard each of the 2 solid-color fabrics for ruffles
1 yard solid-color fabric for 2 plain pillows
Pillow forms, 14 inches muslin-covered
Welting, purchased solid-color, 1¾ yards for each ruffled pillow
Pinking shears

For each ruffled pillow, cut a 15-inch square front and back from floral fabric. Cut tiered ruffle strips the same as for the Balloon Shades, making each about 2½ times the measurement around the pillow. See Two-piece Pillows under General Directions to complete the pillow, adding welting as specified.

Make plain pillows in the same manner, omitting the ruffle and the welting.

Tablecloth

MATERIALS

Fabrics or sheets, one floral and one solid color to match shades, solid color for round bottom cloth and welting (see Circular Tablecloth and Bias Strips under General Directions to estimate yardages), floral for top cloth, and solid color for lining (see instructions to estimate yardages)

Cord, for welting, to fit around both cloths

See Circular Tablecloth under General Directions to cut the bottom cloth from solid-color fabric, adding ½-inch seam allowance. From the solid color, cut bias strips and make corded welting (see General Directions). With right sides facing and raw edges matching, stitch the welting around the cloth. Turn the welting down and topstitch just above the stitching line.

For the top cloth, draw a free-form design (or follow the outline of the flowers) on the wrong side of the floral fabric. The cloth must be large enough to drape over the table as shown. Cut it out, leaving 2 to 3 inches excess. Lightly mark the seamline on the right side. From the solid color cut a lining the same size and make corded welting; pin the welting, with the raw edges facing outward, to the seamline of the floral piece.

With right sides facing and welting sandwiched between, stitch print and lining together, leaving an opening for turning. Trim excess, leaving ¼-inch seam allowance. Clip the curves and turn the cloth right side out. Sew the opening closed.

Note: There are various references to using sheets under General Directions. You may find them helpful in developing this project.

THE VALUE OF TEXTURE

The Roman shade is a trim way to cover a window, and you can add a subtle softness with a batiste fabric shirred from side to side. Pulling it up adds the further texture of ruffles.

MATERIALS
Sheer fabric, such as batiste, about 2½ times wider and 5 inches longer than window
Dowels (slightly shorter than window width), one ¼ inch, several (see instructions) ⅛ inch
Plastic curtain rings (see instructions)
Screw eyes, 3
Thin cord
Bias tape, 1-inch-wide
Wooden strip, ¾ inch × 2 inches × length of dowels
Tacks
Screws or nails to fasten strip
Cord cleat

Fold ½ inch on all edges of the fabric to the wrong side; topstitch. Fold 3 inches more at lower edge to wrong side; topstitch ⅝ inch from fold for the bottom rod pocket. Topstitch 1½ inches and 2⅛ inches above this pocket for a second pocket. Measuring from the second pocket to 1 inch below the upper edge, mark sides of fabric in equal sections (about 5 inches apart for the remaining pockets). Stitch edges and one end of the bias tape across the back of the fabric at marks.

Insert ¼-inch dowel in bottom pocket and smaller dowels in the remaining pockets. Tack ends of pockets closed.

Tack the top of the shade over the wooden strip. In bottom of strip insert screw eyes about 1 inch from each end and a third one at center. Tack the three rings, aligned with the screw eyes, to the back of each pocket (except top and bottom pockets). Tie cord to each bottom ring; pass each cord up through the rings and from right to left through the screw eye directly above; then pass the cord through all screw eyes directly to the left so that they hang together along side of shade.

Tie cords together; trim ends. Screw or nail the wooden strip to the top of the window. Attach the cord cleat to side of window.

DON'T SPARE THE ROD

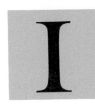 f you decide to decorate a wide window with a freely draped length of sheer material, try encasing a thick rod with a shirred printed fabric. This will keep the sheer material from slipping and bring in an additional design element.

MATERIALS

Fabric for rod: cotton-blend, enough to make a gathered tube to cover curtain rod (1 yard of 45-inch-wide fabric will make a tube about 7 yards long)

Fabric for drape: sheer (see General Directions to estimate yardage with string)

Curtain rod, about 1½-inch-diameter

Cut strips of cotton-blend fabric wide enough to wrap loosely over the rod plus 1 inch. Stitch the strips together end to end to make a length twice as long as the rod. With ½-inch seam allowance, stitch the length in half, right side out, along the long edge, to form a tube. Slide the tube onto the rod, gathering it, and keeping the seam straight. Hang the rod with seam hidden at the back.

Using the photograph as a guide, drape the sheer fabric over the rod.

A FEELING OF MOVEMENT

If you don't want pattern at the window, you can still have drama, achieved here by fastening a loosely woven fabric to four wooden rosettes, letting lovely swooping folds descend.

MATERIALS

Drapery fabric, 54-inch-wide loosely woven fabric (Measure from top of window frame to floor and add desired top and bottom hem allowances.)

Binding fabric, 2 strips of contrasting fabric (we used lightweight canvas), 7 inches wide × 1 inch longer than finished panel length

Finishing nails

Wooden knobs, four 2-inch-diameter

Florist's clay

Curtain rings, 4 small (optional)

Make a narrow hem at top and a wider hem at bottom of the fabric panel.

Depending on desired thickness, either enclose 3 inches at the sides in the binding or make 3-inch extensions (flanges) by stitching a strip to the panel side with right sides together (½-inch seam allowance). Fold the strip in half to wrong side; turn all raw edges in, then sew in place.

Attach the top edge of the panel to the window frame at each end and at two spots evenly spaced between the ends with finishing nails hammered halfway into the frame. To permit removal for cleaning, attach small rings or ties to the top hem of the panel and hang or tie them on the nails. Fill the holes in the knobs with florist's clay. Push knobs onto the nails.

THE DIFFERENCE IS STREAMERS

R eady-made sheers that reach the sills in a sun room do their daylight-controlling job nicely enough, but ribbon streamers and tiebacks add the crucial personal touch.

MATERIALS
Sheer curtains
Ribbons, 1½-inch-wide satin or
    grosgrain, in two colors, 1 yard each
    color for each streamer, 1½ yards each
    color for each tieback
Cup hooks, 1 for each tieback

Hang the curtains. For a streamer, hold together two 1-yard lengths of different-color ribbons; knot them at the center over the end of the curtain rod. Trim ribbon ends diagonally.

For a tieback, hold two 1½-yard lengths of ribbons together, as before, and knot them around a curtain panel. Screw a cup hook into the window frame and hook the tieback over it.

SWAGS AND STREAMERS

This gracefully draped curtain is practically done once you have brought home two flat sheets and some ribbon.

MATERIALS
Sheets, 2 flat printed, twin-size
Ribbon, 2 yards, 2 inches wide
Wooden curtain rod, to fit through
   sheet hem
Curtain hooks, 2

Slide the rod through the wide hems on both sheets. Hang the rod in its brackets, then drape up the sheets in swags as shown, and tie them with ribbon bows. Slip the bows on the curtain hooks, then slide the hooks on the rod.

FROM SHEETS TO COUNTRY CHIC

T he right bed linens are perfectly suitable in the living room. In a few sewing sessions they yield ruffle-skirted slipcovers, pillows, bow-tied chair pads, lampshade covers, and upholstered folding screens.

Slipcover

MATERIALS

Fabrics or sheets, plaid, plus a coordinating solid color for flounce, trim and welting (see instructions to estimate slipcover yardage; see Bias Strips under General Directions to estimate welting yardage)

Cord, for welting (measure edges to be trimmed—see instructions)

Paper, for patterns

Use your old slipcover to make a pattern for your new one, and graph paper to estimate yardage (see General Directions). Cut pieces from plaid fabric. If you do not have a flounce to measure, cut a length of plaid fabric (pieced if necessary) 2½ times longer than the measurement around the sofa and the depth of your sofa-to-floor measurement plus ½-inch hem allowance. For a solid-color border, cut a 4-inch-wide strip the same length as the plaid flounce strip.

Measure all the seams for the amount of welting you will need. See Bias Strips and Corded Welting under General Directions to make the welting.

With right sides facing, the welting sandwiched between, assemble the slipcover pieces in the same manner as they were assembled in the old cover, then make the flounce as follows:

With right sides facing, stitch the border to the bottom of the flounce strip; press the border downward, then topstitch a ½-inch hem. Stitch the strip to form a ring. Adjust the depth if necessary, then gather the top edge to fit around the slipcover. With right sides facing, stitch the flounce around the cover.

Pillows

MATERIALS

Fabrics or sheets, to match slipcover, ⅝ yard plaid, 1⅛ yards solid color

Quilt batting, ½-inch-thick, two 20-inch squares

Pillow forms, 20 inches square, muslin-covered

Cut two 21-inch squares: a plaid front and a solid-color back. Baste the batting to the wrong side of the plaid square. Cut four solid-color strips 4 × 21 inches for the border; press one long edge ½ inch under on each. Pin the borders, right side up, on the right side of the plaid square, raw edges matching and the border corners overlapping. Topstitch the inner pressed edges. Quilt by topstitching along several of the plaid lines.

To assemble the cover, see Two-piece Pillow under General Directions.

Chair Seat and Back

MATERIALS

Fabrics or sheets, to match slipcover, plaid for seat and back, solid color for welting and ties (see instructions to estimate seat and back yardage; see Bias Strips under General Directions to estimate welting yardage)

Cord, for welting, to fit around seat

and back, plus 6 yards for ties
Quilt batting, 1-inch-thick, about twice
    the size of chair seat
Paper, for patterns

Make a paper pattern for seat and chair
back, cutting out notches around the
arms and legs, as shown.

Make the ties first (see Welting Ties
under General Directions). You will
need sixteen 13-inch lengths.

From the patterns, cut two pieces
from the plaid and one from the batting
for each cushion, adding ½-inch seam
allowance all around. See Bias Strips
and Corded Welting under General
Directions to make the welting.

Baste the batting to the wrong side of
each top piece. With raw edges matching, pin the welting to the right side of
each top piece. With the ties lying
inward, pin the raw ends of two ties to
each corner of seat and back top.

With right sides facing and ties sandwiched between, stitch matching pieces
together, leaving an opening for turning; trim seams. Turn pieces right side
out and sew the openings closed.

Lampshade Cover

MATERIALS
Fabric, plaid to match slipcover, ¾ yard

Cut a 25½-inch square from the fabric.
Cut two 3 × 25½-inch strips and two
3 × 26½-inch strips for borders. Turn
the border edges under ½ inch and
press; fold and press the borders in half
lengthwise, right side out. Encase two
opposite sides of the square in the

short borders; topstitch. Repeat with
the long borders on the remaining
sides, turning in the ends and sewing.

For ventilation, cut a 5-inch-diameter
hole in the center of the square. Roll or
topstitch a narrow hem, clipping the
curves. Place the cover over the shade.

Padded Door Screens

MATERIALS
Fabric, plaid to match slipcover, to
    cover both sides of each door, plus
    about 4 inches on each edge
Hollow wooden doors, 4 (ours are 1¾
    inches × 12 inches, × 8 feet high)
Quilt batting, 1-inch-thick, cut to fit one
    side of each door
Brass hinges, 6
Decorative brass upholstery tacks,
    about 116 for each door
Staple gun

Working with one door at a time, cut
and glue batting to the door front. Cut
one piece of fabric 1 inch smaller on
each edge than the door back; cut
another piece to fit over the door front,
sides, and 2 inches onto the back.
Stretch the larger fabric tightly over the
batting and staple it to the back of the
door, folding the corners neatly.

Center and staple the smaller fabric
on the door back, covering the first
staples inserted.

Glue the trim over the exposed stapled edges. Hammer the decorative
tacks as shown, to the front. Repeat the
process with each door. Attach hinges
to pairs of doors.

CLASSICAL GLAMOUR

As softly and deeply pleated as the carved drapery on the statue of a Greek goddess, sheer fabric frames a window elegantly. Topped by a coiled knot and fastened with drapery pins, each panel fans out fluidly on the floor.

MATERIALS

Fabric, sheer (ninon or batiste), 54 inches to 60 inches wide, enough to drape on the floor and gather into a knot at the top end of each panel

Drapery pins, 2

Sturdy sewing thread

Cut fabric in half to form two panels.

Hem the lower end of each, then gather the upper end and coil it into a knot, tying the knot tightly to hold.

Using the drapery pins, attach the coils to each end of your shade valance, allowing each of the panels to fan out onto the floor.

INDOOR AWNING IN CRISP STRIPES

C ut down glare, preserve the view, and give the window a fresh face with a shallow inside awning. Dowel-propped and easy to sew with lace edge and bow-tie corners, this is a conversation piece that starts with common ticking.

MATERIALS

Note: Materials are given for awning 30 × 68 inches to fit 68-inch window. Adjust materials to your requirements.

Fabric, 58-inch-wide, medium-weight ticking, polished cotton, or other sturdy fabric

Lace edging, 2 yards, 2-inch-wide

Dowels, two ½ inch × 36 inches

Lattice strips, two ¼ inch × ⅞ inch × 6 feet (for narrower window, use a tension rod and one lattice strip)

From fabric cut a center panel 32½ × 55 inches, two side extensions 32½ × 8 inches, and four tie strips 5 × 27½ inches.

With right sides together, stitch an extension to each 32½-inch edge of center panel (½-inch seam allowance).

Topstitch ¼-inch finished hem (see General Directions) on the side edges.

Turn one long (lower) edge under ½ inch, then 2 inches, for lattice-strip casing; topstitch. Cut lace 1 inch longer than lower edge. Turn ½ inch under at each end; topstitch long edge over the lower edge of the casing.

Zigzag stitch or hem the raw top edge of the awning. If using a tension rod, turn 1¾ inches under for a rod pocket, then topstitch.

Stitch fabric strips end to end in pairs to make two 5 × 54-inch ties. Fold each tie in half lengthwise; cut the ends diagonally from corner to the fold. Zigzag stitch or seam the raw edges of the ties. Tie each strip into a bow, then tack the bows to the lower corners of the awning.

Cut lattice strip(s) to the width of the awning. Insert into the lower casing. To hang the awning, fold the top edge over the remaining lattice strip and staple or tack it to the window frame through fabric and lattice, or use tension rod. Prop up the corners of the awning with dowels (see photograph).

BLANKETS AND BOWS

For a curtain that helps you keep the heat inside and the cold outside, take an open-weave thermal blanket, thread it with ribbons, and tie it with bows.

MATERIALS
Thermal blanket, open-weave
Ribbon, the width of openings in blanket (see instructions to estimate yardage) and 1½ yards of 6-inch-wide ribbon for tiebacks
Safety pin, large
Curtain rod
Curtain ring, small
Cup hook

To estimate the ribbon yardage, spread the blanket out flat, then plan where you want to weave the ribbons. Our ribbons are woven in wide (6-ribbon) horizontal bands and narrow (1-ribbon) vertical bands. Measure the planned stripes to determine the ribbon yardage for the bands.

For bows, tie a scrap of ribbon or yarn into a bow of desired size; untie it and measure the length. Multiply this figure by the number of bows you plan.

Fold the blanket over the curtain rod to the desired length, with the overhang forming a valance. Mark the fold, remove the blanket, and spread it out flat again. Weave the ribbons through the holes on the blanket with a safety pin, being sure to weave the valance area on the *reverse* side. Fold the blanket on the fold line and topstitch a rod casing. Slide the curtain onto the rod and hang. Loop it back with the wide ribbon tied into a bow. Sew the curtain ring to the ribbon and hang it on the cup hook screwed into the window frame.

THE OLD HOUSE

Quirky problems abound in great old houses, but there are always imaginative solutions to be found, and these often produce window treatments to enhance any house.

READYMADES DRESS TRICKY WINDOWS

French doors and a fanlight-crowned window are decorating problems in themselves; here both are in one room. The solution: sheer voile purchased curtains on window and door, plus satin jabots at the fan window.

Fan Window

MATERIALS

Voile under-curtains: 2 panels for lower fan window, 1 panel for fan
Antique satin draperies: 2 panels for side jabots on lower window, 1 panel for rod pocket and ruching
Curved rod for fan (designer used malleable copper tubing attached to wall with screws)
Straight rods, 2 to span lower window

For fan, make rod casing 2 inches in from one long edge of a panel. Gather the panel on the curved rod, pull the excess together at lower center, and sew gathers into a bunch. Cut excess away, leaving just enough for a neat rosette shape made by folding the ends under and tacking them to center of the frame.

Hang under-curtains on a single rod.

Cut lower ends of the draperies on the diagonal, as shown, and rehem. A band of ruching, cut from the extra panel, can be added along the center front and diagonal edges. To do this, cut strips about 4 inches wide, fold in half lengthwise, gather, then stitch to the panel edges.

To cover the center of the straight rod, from the extra panel cut and stitch a loose rod pocket 1½ times the length of the rod. Gather it onto the center of the rod, then slide the side panels onto the same rod.

French Doors

MATERIALS

Voile under-curtains, 3 panels
Hooks, 10 small decorative plant hooks with screw ends

Screw the hooks into the frame above the glass panels, spacing them evenly. For hanging loops, cut ten 4 × 6-inch lengths from the extra panel. Hem the ends. Fold lengthwise, stitch with ½-inch seam allowance and use a safety pin to turn them right side out. Fold the lengths in half crosswise and stitch, spacing them evenly, to the back of the remaining two panel headings. Hang panels from hooks.

ROMANTIC SHUTTERS

Put up a Quaker lace curtain, attach the measured pieces to ready-made interior shutters, and you will get adjustable privacy, lasting charm, and fascinating light patterns when the sun shines in.

MATERIALS

Unfinished shutter frames (home centers have single frames in assorted sizes that can be hinged to form bifold shutters, as shown)

Narrow molding strips, to fit around inner edge of each frame

Finishing nails

Paint or stain

Quaker lace curtains, as needed to fill frames

White glue

Apply finish (paint or stain) to the frames and molding strips. From a lace curtain, cut panels 1 inch wider and 1 inch longer than the opening in the frame. Glue the panels to the wrong side of the frames, then cover raw edges with the molding strips and nail them in place.

ATTIC TREASURE SEES THE LIGHT

An heirloom linen tablecloth found in a trunk, freshly laundered and pressed, can simply fold over a rod for a special window heading. If you like the look and lack the heirloom, there are new ones you can buy.

MATERIALS
Lacy tablecloth, round or oval, the
   width of window
Curtain rod

Fold the cloth over the rod with the back edge a little lower than the front, as shown. Tack in place; or mark the fold, remove the cloth, and topstitch a rod casing at the marking. Then slide the cloth back on the rod and hang.

FLAUNT A SPECIAL FEATURE

N o law says curtains have to hang from the top of the frame. Here a decorative leaded pane remains in view over a balloon shade and under a valance.

MATERIALS
Voile under-curtains, 2 pinch-pleated
   panels
Voile balloon shade
Moiré draperies, 2 panels each, rose
   and camel
Tiebacks, 3 × 44 inches, 2 rose and 6
   camel
Window scarf, rose (to drape as shown)
Rods, 2 for each side window, 1 for
   balloon shade, 1 curved rod with 5-
   inch return at ends for scarf
Hooks, 2

Hang the balloon shade from a rod spanning the molding that separates the two center windows.

   Hang the voile under-curtains, then on separate rod at each side, hang one moiré panel of each color.

   Drape with rose tiebacks placed high, fastening the tiebacks to the window frame with hooks. Tie ends in an overhand knot, then loosely knot a camel tieback over the rose tieback.

   Slide the window scarf over the curved rod, tacking it into loops, as shown, with a few stitches.

   To make rosettes, cut the remaining four camel tiebacks in half crosswise. Sew ends of one half together to form a ring. Gather one edge, pull up the stitches, and fasten to form a rosette. Fold other half of tieback in half crosswise; draw the raw ends, from front to back, through the hole on rosette, leaving the folded end showing. Sew in place. Tie ends extending from back of rosette around the rod.

THE RETURN OF THE LACE CURTAIN

Lace is fresh and airy and creates instant nostalgia—no wonder it has made such a comeback. Ready-made lace panels are easy to find these days. Floating over glass, draped into swag-and-jabot headings, lace suits any room in the house.

MATERIALS

Fabrics for curtain: lace curtain panel or tablecloth for glass curtain, light-weight fabric or another tablecloth or panel for swag to drape as shown.

Fabric for streamer ties: fabric to match wallpaper or another coordinating fabric, 4 inches wide × 45 inches long for each streamer

Curtain rod

Cup hooks, 2

Fasten the curtain rod near the top of the window frame and hang the lace curtain panel; if using a tablecloth, cut it 3 inches longer than the desired length and stitch a rod pocket at the cut end. Slide the panel on the rod.

Screw a cup hook into each upper corner of the window frame. To make a streamer tie, fold a 4 × 45-inch piece of fabric in half lengthwise, wrong side out; stitch one end and the long edge, with ½-inch seam allowance. Trim the seam and, with the help of a closed safety pin, turn the length right side out; sew the end closed. Knot two lengths around the swag fabric, then slip the knots over the cup hooks.

ACCENTS

S oft touches in small doses can brighten a room like a new piece of jewelry. Larger accessories can set the mood and character of a room, and the inventive ways to make these various miracle-workers are numberless.

SOUTHWESTWARD HO

Capture the newly popular Southwestern look with pillows covered in characteristic hot colors and interesting weaves. Instead of ordinary yard goods, use place mats, shawls, shoulder bags, and other gift finds.

MATERIALS
Fabrics, homespun-type or ticking in neutral colors (see instructions to estimate yardage)
Appliqués, woven folk bands, and other bright fabrics
Cord, ⅜-inch-diameter for welting
Pillow forms, desired size

Basic Pillow Cover
(except Flange-edged, opposite)
See Three-piece Pillow under General Directions to make cover, applying trims to the front piece (see opposite) and inserting any corded welting (see General Directions).

Special Trims: Use woven bands, or cut wide or narrow strips of colorful fabric and turn the raw edges under.
Topstitch bands to cover the front across the center, in a grid or as a border with mitered corners (see General Directions), positioning heavy fabrics to avoid seams.

Flange-edged Pillow Cover
We used a hemmed 17½-inch square napkin for front, a fringed 22-inch square napkin for back (or cut your own 18-inch and 22-inch squares, hemming the smaller square and fringing the other square). With fabrics right side out, center the pillow form on the large napkin, cover it with the small napkin; pin in place. Topstitch around the edge of small napkin, using zipper foot to stitch close to pillow.

PRACTICAL AND PRETTY

To hide stereo equipment, radiators, or a tangle of wires, you might want to make this hinged screen as a room accent or divider sporting a colorful shirred fabric.

Size: Each frame is about 18 × 26 inches.

MATERIALS
Wood strips, 11/16-inch square, eight
    16 × 26 inches for 4 frames
Lattice, eight ¼ × ⅞ × 18-inch strips
Fabric, 54-inch-wide cotton-blend print,
    1½ yards
Butt hinges with screws, six 2-inch
Wood screws, sixteen ¾-inch
Finishing nails, 2-inch
Nail set
Wood glue
Wood putty
Scrap wood or miter box
Primer
Semigloss paint

To make each frame, glue and nail two 16-inch strips between two 26-inch strips, placing one 16-inch strip ¾ inch from one end (bottom) and the other 1¾ inches from opposite end (top) of the 26-inch strips. Sink nails and fill holes. Sand, prime, and paint.

Join the frames in pairs with two hinges each, attaching the plates to the back of the frames. Then join the pairs with two hinges, attaching the plates to the sides of frames with hinges toward the front, so that the screen will stand in a zigzag position.

Stand the lattice strips, for curtain rods, on edge against scrap wood or in a miter box; trim ends ⅛ inch, making diagonal cuts toward each other.

Cut four pieces of fabric 26 inches long × 27 inches wide with the pattern

vertical. Press 26-inch sides under ¼ inch then ½ inch; topstitch. Press 27-inch ends under ¼ inch then 1¼ inches for casings; topstitch along first folds. Gather the casings on the lattice strips so that the right side of the fabric and the longer face of the strip will face the front of the screen. Place the strips behind the crosspieces on the frame and screw the ends in place.

ALL THE TRIMMINGS

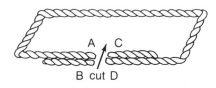

Passementerie, the official name for luxurious trims, is an essential part of the Victorian style, shown here on elegant pillows embellished with cords and fringes from upholstery suppliers.

MATERIALS

Fabric, decorator types such as chintz, brocade, or jacquard (see instructions to estimate yardage)

Trim, decorator's heavy round cord, fringed trim, or tassels, in combinations of 2 or 3 as shown in photograph

Clear plastic tape, craft knife, white glue, waxed paper, and cardboard (all for joining ends of round cord)

Pillow forms, muslin-covered, desired size

See Three-piece Pillow under General Directions to make a basic pillow cover to fit your pillow form.

Hand-sew cords, fringes, or tassels, in combinations of two or three, to the seamline and to pillow front, easing around corners.

To finish round cord ends neatly, work as follows: Pin cord to the pillow cover. Where ends overlap (match pattern on striped cord), remove pins from the cover. Wrap the lapped ends tightly together with clear tape for about 2 inches. With craft knife, make a diagonal slice through the tape and cord (see diagram). Put a drop of white glue on raw ends A and D; pin them to waxpaper-covered cardboard until the joint is secure. Peel away the tape and remove ends B and C.

FROM FIRELIGHT TO FLOWERLIGHT

ne way to screen a dormant fireplace is with an expensive, hard-to-find antique fireboard; another is to create a fireboard of your own out of plywood, covered with a riot of cut-out chintz flowers in a basket made from a complementary geometric print.

Size: About 32 inches high × 36 inches wide

MATERIALS

Densely printed floral chintz, 1½ to 2 yards
Scrap of contrasting fabric for basket and stands
Smooth ¾-inch plywood, 3-foot square
Black paint (any kind)
Paintbrush, 3-inch
Mod Podge® decoupage sealer-glue and 2-inch brush
Artist's spray adhesive (optional)
Wood putty
Sandpaper, assorted
Paper, large sheet for pattern
Finishing nails, four 2-inch
Double-faced tape
Craft knife
Jigsaw or band saw

Cut flowers and leaves from the floral fabric and arrange a bouquet roughly 27 × 36 inches wide on paper, overlapping the flowers as desired. Pin or tape the pieces together as arranged. Draw an outline of the floral arrangement on paper to make a pattern, adding a basket shape at the bottom (see photograph).

Slide the pattern from under the fabric and cut it out, adding ⅛-inch around all edges except around the basket edges. Cut out ¾-inch-wide × 2-inch-high notch at the bot-

tom of the basket, 3 inches in from each side, for inserting the stands in the bottom of the basket.

Make a separate rectangular pattern for the stands, 3½ inches high × 8 inches long with a corresponding notch in the center of one long edge (top); shape top corners in a curve.

Trace the patterns for the screen and two stands onto plywood and cut out with jigsaw or band saw. Fill any voids

at the edges with wood putty, then sand smooth. Paint edges and both sides of all pieces; let dry.

Cut basket fabric slightly larger than the area to be covered. Spray adhesive on the back of the fabric. Press and smooth the fabric by hand over the screen. Turn the screen over and cut off excess fabric with the craft knife. Cover both sides of the stands in the same manner.

Starting with outer underlying flower pieces, apply Mod Podge or spray glue to back of flowers and press them onto the screen. Attach flowers in this manner, section by section, then layer by layer. Finally, coat with Mod Podge.

Matching the notches, slide stands in place at screen bottom. Toenail through top edge of stands into the screen. Paint over the nailheads.

FAMILY ALBUM SCREEN

Over quilt batting you simply cut, glue, and staple sheet fabric on a purchased three-panel screen. Then, let your sentimental impulses take over, hanging favorite pictures on ribbons topped with flat bows.

MATERIALS
Screen, wooden-framed three-panel (each panel about 13 × 72 inches)
Fabric, king-size sheet or 6¼ yards of 36-inch-wide or 45-inch-wide tightly woven fabric
Quilt batt, 81 × 96 × ½-inch
Ribbon, 19 yards of ⅝-inch-wide grosgrain
White glue
Staple gun

Remove hinges from the screen. Cut the quilt batt into six 13 × 72-inch rectangles or to fit the screen panel. Applying glue lightly here and there, glue a batt to both sides of each panel.

Cut fabric into three 32 × 75-inch pieces. With a helper, wrap each around a panel, overlapping the long edges at the frame edge (mark location of hinge screw holes). Stretching fabric tightly, staple it along the center of the frame edge. Lap the top edges, folding corners neatly; staple. Repeat with bottom edges. Trim excess fabric about ¼ inch from the staples.

Starting at center bottom, wrap ribbon around the frame, gluing it over the staples. (Spread glue lightly on the fabric, not on the ribbon, and mark the hinge screw holes.) Reattach the hinges, screwing through the ribbon and the fabric.

A BRITISH IDEA

Pictures in English country houses often hang on ribbons topped with a bow or, like this one, a rosette. For real impact, hang more than one picture in a room this way.

MATERIALS
Upholstery trim, 3¼-inch-wide, 2¼ yards
Heavy-duty thread
Bottle cap, 1½-inch-diameter
Small plastic ring
Masking tape
Hooks, 2 (one for hanging picture, one for hanging rosette trim)

From trim cut two 19-inch lengths for streamers and a 29-inch length for rosette. Cut a 3-inch-diameter circle from scrap; cover the bottle cap with the circle and gather the edges tightly with running stitch, securing thread on the underside of the cap.

Sew the ends of the 29-inch strip together. Gather and sew one long edge in accordion pleats to form a rosette around the covered cap. Tack the gathered edge to the underside of the cap.

Tack one end of each streamer to the back of the rosette, forming an inverted V to fit the picture. Sew the small ring to the back of the rosette for hanging. Tape the loose ends of the tails to the back of the picture, just above the picture wire (streamers and rosette should hide the wire). Hang the picture, then hang the rosette above from a separate hook. Rosette does not support the picture.

QUILTING AS ART

C rib quilts—often more expensive antiques than those in full sizes—make terrific wall art, and when you are sewing the squares, stitch up a few more for pillows.

Crib Quilt

Size: 37 × 54 inches

MATERIALS

Fabrics, 45-inch-wide cotton blend: 2 yards green print (includes backing); ½ yard each blue print and burgundy print; ¾ yard unbleached muslin

Quilt batt, 38 × 55 inches × 1 inch thick

Crochet cotton, thin, for tufting, about 20 yards

Large-eyed yarn needle

Wooden lattice, 1¼ × 54-inch strip

Picture wire

Cardboard and tracing paper to make patterns

Seam allowance of ¼ inch is included in the measurements for the quilt. Label the pieces with letters as indicated on the Patchwork and Assembly diagrams.

Cutting: For backing, starting at a corner of the fabric, cut one piece 42 × 59 inches. For borders, from backing fabric cut two strips (A) 1½ × 51 inches, two strips (B) 1½ × 33 inches, two strips (C) 2½ × 33½ inches, three strips (D) 2½ × 15½ inches.

For patchwork square (make 6): Enlarge patterns E and F (see General Directions). Cut patterns from cardboard for templates. Draw around the templates on wrong side of fabric, then add ¼ inch all around for seam allowance. Cut 4 E pieces from burgundy print and 8 F

pieces from blue. Then cut pieces as follows: four 2¼-inch green-print squares (G), five 2¼-inch burgundy squares (H), two 5⅞-inch muslin squares, and four 2⅞-inch muslin squares. Cut each muslin square in half diagonally to form four large triangles (I) and eight small triangles (J).

To assemble square: Following the Patchwork Diagram, stitch the nine center squares together; stitch J triangles to F strips; stitch the F/J and E strips together, then stitch to the nine-square center block. Add I triangles. Press seam allowances to one side.

To assemble front: Following the Assembly Diagram, stitch D borders to squares, then C borders in place; stitch B side borders and A end borders around quilt.

To finish: With wrong sides facing, place front on back with the batt centered between. Pin the layers together.

To tuft: Thread a double-strand of crochet cotton through the large-eyed needle. Following the dots on the Patchwork Diagram, take a small stitch from the front through all layers; tie a square knot on front and trim the ends to 1-inch.

Trim batt, if necessary, so that it extends about 1½ inches beyond each edge of front. Lap side edges of the backing over to the front; turn raw edges under and topstitch. Fold and stitch the end edges in the same manner as before, mitering the corners (see General Directions).

To use quilt as wall hanging: With heavy thread, sew the lattice strip across the top back edge of the quilt by

winding thread around the strip after each stitch. Add wire, pull it taut, and hang the quilt as you would a picture. Or fasten the lattice strip to the wall with appropriate wall fasteners.

Pillow

Size: 16-inch square

MATERIALS (for one)

Fabrics, 45-inch-wide cotton blend: ½ yard green print; ⅛ yard each blue print and burgundy print or quilt scraps; ¼ yard unbleached muslin

Pillow form, 16-inch, muslin-covered

Zipper, 14-inch

Cardboard and tracing paper to make patterns

Make one patchwork square as for the quilt (vary colors if desired). Cut a 17-inch square of backing fabric. From same fabric cut two 1¼ × 15½-inch side borders and two 1¼ × 17-inch end borders (¼-inch seam allowance included). Stitch the side borders to the square, then stitch top and bottom borders. Join the top of front to back with the zipper centered on one edge. Stitch remaining edges of back and front together; clip corners. Turn right side out. Insert the pillow form.

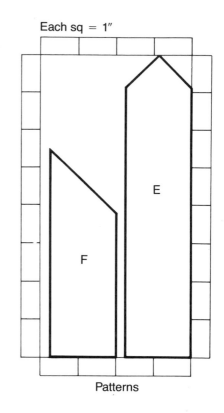

Each sq = 1″

Patterns

Finished size is 15″.

Patchwork Diagram

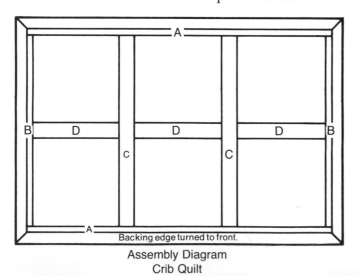

Backing edge turned to front.

Assembly Diagram
Crib Quilt

DRESSING UP PLAIN PILLOWS

To get a provincial look in minutes, make yourself some instant patchwork by simply tacking printed napkins or scarves diagonally to ready-made solid-color pillows.

MATERIALS
Fabrics, pretty scarves, or napkins that fit diagonally on pillows
Pillows or muslin-covered pillow forms

Pin a scarf or napkin directly over the pillow, turning the corners under, if necessary, at the pillow seams. Hand-sew in place.

EASY-SEW SOFT-TOUCH APPLIQUÉ

To achieve this delicate, misty appliqué effect, make a collage of cut-out fabric flowers with batting attached, then sew the petals in place through a cover of transparent organza.

MATERIALS
Cover fabrics: solid-color cotton blend, 2 pieces to cover pillow, plus ½-inch seam allowance
Floral print, for appliqué
Organza, 1 piece, same size as cover
Quilt batting, 1 piece, to cover pillow front

Pillow form, muslin-covered, desired size

Spread the batting on a flat surface, then place the cover top, right side up, on the batting. With sharp scissors, carefully cut out floral motifs from the print; arrange and pin them on the cover. Place the organza over the cover; pin, then baste the layers together.

See General Directions for a Two-piece Pillow to complete the cover.

DRESS-UP LAMPSHADE

Perk up a ho-hum lampshade by slip-covering it in a pretty fabric that you softly pleat and ruffle. Not only will this be a charming decorative note, but it will also produce a romantically muted light.

MATERIALS
Fabric (see instructions to estimate
    yardage)
Pinking shears

For cover, cut a strip of fabric about 3 inches shorter than height of shade and about twice as long as bottom circumference. Trim one long edge (top) with pinking shears.

For ruffle, cut 4-inch-wide strip with pinking shears 1½ times as long as cover strip, piecing if necessary.

Gather the ruffle strip ½ inch from edge to fit the cover strip. Topstitch ruffle on the gathering line to the cover ½ inch from the lower edge. Stitch ends of the cover to form a ring.

Gather top of the cover ½ inch from edge to fit the lampshade so that the gathered edge sits about ½ inch above the shade. Topstitch along the gathering line to secure the stitches. Slip the cover over the shade.

SLIPCOVERED BASKET

A terrific use for leftover fabric is this pleated basket cover. You need enough material for the inside, the outside, and the handle, plus a yard or two of ribbon to glue to the edge.

MATERIALS
Fabric, to cover handle and inside and outside of basket (see instructions to estimate yardage)

Lace, 1½-inch-wide, to circle basket rim twice and to wind spirally around handle, plus 3 yards for bows
Ribbon, ½-inch-wide picot-edge satin, 3 yards each pink and green
Batting, to fit around outer side of basket
Old sheet or scrap fabric
White glue

To estimate fabric yardage, use an old

sheet or large pieces of scrap fabric. Follow instructions to cut sample pieces to cover your basket, then use these pieces as patterns.

Cut batting to fit around the basket; overlap ends and sew them together.

Set the basket on the wrong side of the center of a large piece of fabric; bring the fabric up and over the basket rim to bottom of inside, folding and pleating it to fit. Mark fabric where it laps about 2 inches onto inside bottom. Unfold the fabric, spread it out and cut a large circle, following the marks.

Set the basket in center of the circle. Smear white glue on the inside of the basket, then bring the circle up and over the rim as before, pleating it neatly and finger-pressing it against the glued sides. Let dry.

Cut a fabric circle to fit inside the basket bottom, generously covering raw edges of the cover. Turn the circle edges under and sew or glue them to the bottom of basket.

Cut 2-inch-wide fabric strips, stitching them together as necessary, to spiral around entire handle. Turn the edges under about ½ inch and wrap the strip around the handle, overlapping edges. Secure the ends between the pleats of the cover. Wrap a length of lace around the fabric wrapping.

Cut lace twice the circumference of the basket rim; gather it to fit around the rim. Sew in place.

Cut the ribbons and remaining lace in half. From each length make a four-loop bow with streamers. Sew a lace bow, centered with a pink and green bow, to the outside at ends of handle.

To display fresh flowers, place a deep aluminum pan or ceramic bowl in the basket. Fill it with florist foam and water. Trim the flower stems and insert them into the foam.

NEW LIFE FOR OLD LAMPS

I f a lamp base bores you, don't dump it, just bag it in a fabric that pleases you. Form and pin pleats, then tie it all together with a necklace of cord.

MATERIALS
Old lamp, ginger jar, or jug shape
Fabric, circle large enough to cover
  lamp base plus ¾ inch all around
Decorative cord, 2 yards
White glue (optional)

Place the lamp in the center of the fabric circle and gather the fabric up around the neck. Slit fabric from top down to where the lamp cord emerges, then remove the fabric from the lamp.

Press ¾ inch to wrong side all around the fabric circle. (No need to hem.) Replace the fabric circle on the lamp and pin the top into pleats to fit the neck, lapping edges of the slit and folding the raw edge under. This arrangement depends on the shape of the lamp. (Experiment—you may be able simply to gather the fabric and tie it with a cord.)

Wrap cord around the neck of lamp and tie a knot. Add glue to hold the cord in place if necessary.

STAGE SETS FOR ENTERTAINING

Your dining room or outdoor eating area is a kind of stage set, a place for birthday parties, for the celebration of holidays, family feasts, and sparkling conversation. They are places where you can allow your creativity to function most freely.

POUFS IN THEIR PLACE

How to dress a deep bay window without cutting off a garden view? Hang traditional French poufs—double ones tied with self-bows—on rods covered with shirring. You can use purchased panels or make your own.

MATERIALS

Drapery panels, textured, white, 50 inches wide and about 24 inches longer than rod-to-floor measurement, number of panels needed plus shorter one to cut up for rod pockets

Tiebacks, four 4 × 44 inches for each panel

Ribbon, 1-inch-wide and about 1½ times the rod-to-floor measurement for each panel

Rods, 1 for each window

From short drapery panel, for each rod, cut and stitch a loose-fitting rod pocket about 1½ times the length of the rod. Gather a pocket onto the center of each of the rods. Butt pairs of tiebacks end to end and whipstitch.

Cut ribbon into equal lengths, one for each panel. Sew end of each length to the center of the header on back of each panel, letting ribbon hang down the back. Hang panels as shown, pushed to the ends of the rods with pockets gathered between the panels. Tie two tiebacks tightly in bows around each panel; pull the panel up into two poufs, hem resting on the floor.

To hold poufs in place, pull the ribbon fairly taut and tack it to back of top bow. Cut away excess ribbon, then sew the end of cutaway strip to the panel header just above the first ribbon. Pull taut and sew to the back of the lower bow.

MAKING A PORCH LIVABLE

Some basic sewing is required for the ruffled pillows and chaise back, but the seat cushions are a tuck-and-tie effort that is entirely stitchless. In no time at all, you can enjoy the welcome of an outdoor room.

MATERIALS
Fabric or sheets, floral (see instructions
   to estimate yardage)
Old sheet or scrap fabric
Cushions to be covered

Practice covering a cushion, as specified below, with an old sheet or scrap fabric; then untie and use this piece as a pattern. With the scrap pattern you can determine the amount of fabric you will need for the number of cushions you plan to cover.

   To start, place your cushion bottom side up on the wrong side of fabric or sheet (see diagram). Measure the cushion thickness and draw a line this

distance from the cushion all around (broken line on diagram). Add another 8 inches all around and draw outer line. For example, if cushion is 3 inches high, broken line should be 3 inches from cushion and the outer line should

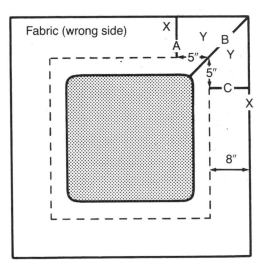

be 8 inches from broken line. Cut around the outer line. Now draw lines A, B, and C at each corner and cut along them. Wrap the fabric over the sides of the cushion. Tie corners X together in a tiny square knot at the bottom of the cushion, pulling fabric as smoothly as possible over the cushion. (You may have to untie and adjust these knots to fit.) Now tie Y sections together in square knots and let the ends hang at corners.

GARAGE GALA

Emergency measure if rain threatens your lawn party: Turn the garage into a festive tent with sheets, cords, and staples. More sheets are draped and tied on tables to carry out the theme.

MATERIALS
Sheets, flat for hangings, fitted for
    tables (see instructions to determine
    quantity)
Decorative cord
Staple gun
Balloons, helium-filled (optional)

Clear the garage of grease or oil; sweep and hose it clean. (Hint: Use cat litter to absorb grease.)

With the door in closed position, measure the entire inner side of the garage to determine the number of flat sheets needed. Staple the sheets over the walls and garage door, then pull up the door to form a ceiling "canopy."

To hide storage units and eyesores, simply bunch and tie flat sheet borders at center and corners with colored cord, then staple or tack the cord to ceiling or beams. (Note: If fasteners do not hold in the plaster, nail lath to ceiling through the plaster into the beams, usually located every 16 inches on center, then staple the cord to lath.)

Cover each table with a fitted sheet and knot corners together.

If you have a center structural column, as this owner did, just wrap and tack a sheet around it, then attach balloons to the center tie.

CHINTZ-LINED BOWER

 bolt of chintz, a length of tiny-checked cotton, a staple gun, a sewing machine, and you can turn an ordinary window corner into a luxurious place for breakfast, tea, or midnight supper.

Yardage instructions for 54-inch-wide fabric are included under each item.

Window Treatment

MATERIALS
Print fabric
Thin flannel, interlining for side trumpets and swag on pole
Fabric, tiny check for pole and for lining trumpets
White lining fabric, for draperies
Wooden drapery pole
Staple gun

For draperies cut tiny-check fabric to cover the pole; fold over the pole and staple to the back.

For each floor-length drapery, use full width of print fabric and cut long enough to fold about 6 inches over pole. Cut lining to fit draperies, piecing if necessary. For swag, cut print fabric and flannel lining 28 × 84 inches (or length that will drape as shown over your rod). Pin flannel to wrong side of print fabric. Fold in half lengthwise, flannel side out; stitch with ½-inch seam allowance; turn right side out. Gather ends. Drape around pole, stapling ends to back of pole.

Line draperies by pinning drapery fabric and lining together, right sides facing; stitch together with ½-inch seam allowance, leaving the lower edge open. Turn right side out. Hem bottom.

Tack top into pleats; fold 6 inches over pole and staple.

For each trumpet cut print, tiny check, and flannel strips 16 inches wide × 6 inches longer than half the window length. Taper to 13 inches at top. Pin flannel for body to wrong side of tiny-check lining. Shape the widest end to rounded point as shown. Using the point as a pattern, cut an inverted point (or wedge) in the wide end of the print piece. Fold lining in half lengthwise, flannel side out, and stitch. Seam print piece the same way. With right sides facing, stitch lining and print tubes together around shaped end; turn right side out. Fold 6 inches of upper end over the rod, and staple.

Tablecloth

MATERIALS
Fabrics, one for top cloth and ruffle, one for bottom cloth and ruffle
Welting cord, to fit around top cloth

For bottom cloth, cut a circle (see General Directions). Cut a 7-inch-wide ruffle strip twice the circumference of the cloth. Stitch ends together and topstitch ½-inch hem along each edge. Gather along center to fit cloth; topstitch to cloth along gathering line.

For top cloth, cut a print square large enough to drape over the table as shown. Baste welting (see General Directions) to the cloth. Cut 8-inch-wide ruffle strip, stitch ends together, and hem one edge. Pleat the raw edge to fit the cloth. With right sides facing, pin to the cloth with welting sandwiched between; stitch.

UPHOLSTERED DINING ROOM

N ot just a treat for the eyes, but for the ears as well, is an inviting dining room whose dado and broad window frame are padded (which muffles sound) and upholstered with attractive sheeting.

MATERIALS
Fabric, full-size flat sheets (we used 2)
Quilt batting, thin, to cover lambrequin and dado
Plasterboard, 12 inches wide and long enough to fit the top and sides of the window
Finishing nails, 1½-inch
Staple gun

Lambrequin
Cut three plasterboard pieces to fit top and sides of the window frame, cutting mitered corners (see photograph). Cut batting 2 inches larger than plasterboard on all sides and staple to the back. Cut fabric 3 inches larger than the plasterboard pieces on all sides.

Stretch the fabric over the batting and staple to the back. Nail the three lambrequin pieces, through the fabric, directly into the window frame, easing the fabric carefully over the nailheads.

Dado
Measure fabric for the wall and cut out the pieces, allowing 1-inch fold allowance on all edges. Staple a layer of batting to the wall between the baseboard and the molding. Fold under and iron the raw edges of the fabric, at top, bottom, and sides, and staple very close to the molding, baseboards, and corners.

CUSTOMIZING READY-MADE SHADES

T he hard part is done by the makers of the balloon shades. The extra fantasy fillip is yours: draping and puffing voile through rings to cascade to the floor at the corners.

MATERIALS
Balloon shades, floral print
Fabric, 60-inch-wide voile (see instructions and General Directions to estimate yardage with string)
Wooden curtain rings, large, 1 for each pouf

First hang the balloon shades, then insert a pin where you want each pouf, being sure to place one at each corner. Fabric should be long enough to pull through the rings into poufs and ends should puddle on the floor.

Sew a wooden ring at each pin, then arrange the fabric across the shades and pull enough voile through each ring to make a pouf, as shown.

THE KITCHEN AS PEOPLE-CENTER

**W**here does the family gather to begin their busy days? Where do they meet again as evening draws them back together? Where do you like to sit with your telephone and your pile of mail? Where does your best friend visit with you over the coffee cups? Chances are the vital people-center in your house is the breakfast room or the eating corner of the kitchen—or it could be if you gave it a cozy redecoration. With the same old furniture, your breakfast area will come to life with a new wall treatment, fresh curtains, or pretty tablecloths and mats.

NEW SLANT ON PLACE MATS

These diagonally pieced mats are easier than they look because you stitch your strips straight, then cut them on a slant. Lined with thin batting, they are machine-quilted to calico backing.

MATERIALS
For four place mats and napkins:
Fabric, ½ yard each of six 45-inch-wide cotton-blend prints for place mats, and 3 yards more of one print for napkins, backing, and bias binding
Quilt batt, thin, 27 × 36 inches
Heavy paper, 13½ × 18 inches to make pattern

Place Mats
From each of the six prints, cut 45-inch-long strips in varied widths of 1¾ inches, 2 inches, and 2¼ inches (includes ¼-inch seam allowance). Stitch strips together to produce 45 × 45-inch striped patchwork.

With paper pattern placed diagonally on the patchwork, cut out four mats. Cut same size backs from one print and interlinings from batting.

With front and back right sides out and batting sandwiched between, topstitch along seamlines. From one print cut 2-inch-wide bias binding (see General Directions) and stitch it around the edge of each mat.

Napkins
Cut 17½-inch print square. Topstitch ½-inch finished hem around square. (See General Directions.)

CHECKMATES

This breakfast corner proves that you can't have too many checks. Here one check borders a curtain and forms seat cushions; a smaller one serves as a tablecloth and is embroidered with a third check. Painted checks decorate wall and wooden bowl; machine-quilted checks cover a pillow.

Tablecloth
Size: Embroidery, 24¾-inch square on 9-squares-to-2-inches gingham.

MATERIALS
Fabric, 45-inch-wide even-weave check with 9 squares to 2 inches, the desired size for tablecloth plus 1-inch hem allowance
Embroidery floss, six-strand, 25 skeins white, 5 red
Embroidery needle
Embroidery hoop

Note: Wash a scrap of red floss with a scrap of your fabric to make sure color will not run.

With basting stitches, mark off a 24¾-inch square in the center of cloth; outer edges should be rows of colored, not white, squares.

Embroider the cloth in chicken-scratch stitch (also called Smyrna cross), using all six strands of floss. Each stitch covers one square. Always stitch white over the shaded squares and solid-color squares, red over the shaded squares only. To work the stitch, follow the Chicken-Scratch Diagram: Bring thread up at 1, down at 2, up at 3, down at 4 (X formed), up at 5, down at 6, up at 7, down at 8 (cross formed over X). The Motif Chart (each square equals one gingham square) shows the basic white and red motifs at the lower right corner of the square. The embroidery design shows the placement of motifs on the tablecloth.

When embroidery is completed, top-stitch a ½-inch finished hem (see General Directions).

Bordered Curtains and Chair Pad

MATERIALS
Fabric, 45-inch-wide white cotton and checked cotton with 1-inch checks (see instructions to estimate yardage)
Quilt batt, thick, for chair pad
Piping, red, to go around chair pad
Pinking shears (optional), for curtain
Curtain rod

To estimate curtain yardage, for the white fabric measure the width of the window (or curtain rod if wider) and add 4-inch hem allowance; measure the desired total curtain length and 2½-inch seam allowance, then subtract 8 inches for the border. (The curtains will be gathered only when the panel is cut in two and separated, as shown.) For checked border, you will need a strip 8 inches long and the same width as the white curtain.

For the chair pad, draw a pattern from the chair seat for the correct size of the cushions, then add ½-inch seam allowance all around. Mark dots and back seamline for the positions of two ties. For each pad you will need fabric twice the size of the pattern, plus a 1½ × 30-inch piece for each tie, and three 3 layers of batting.

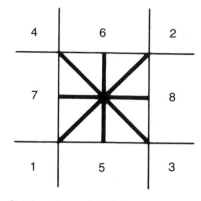

Chicken-Scratch Stitch

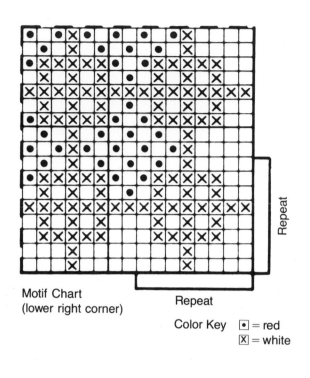

Motif Chart
(lower right corner)

Repeat

Repeat

Color Key   • = red
            X = white

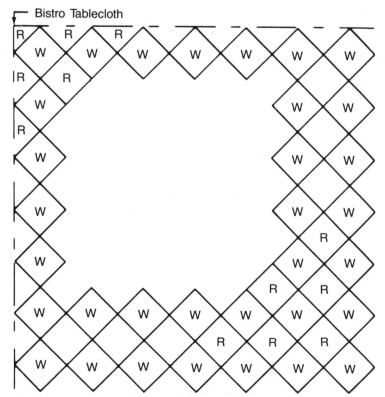

Bistro Tablecloth

Curtains: Cut white cotton curtain and checked border. With right sides together, and allowing ½ inch for seam, stitch the border to the lower edge of the white curtain. Press seam allowances downward; finish the seam edge with pinking shears or zigzag stitching.

Topstitch a ¼-inch finished hem (see General Directions) at the lower edge of the curtain, then cut the curtain in half lengthwise to make a pair. Topstitch ½-inch finished hem at side edges.

Make a rod pocket by folding ½ inch at upper edge to wrong side, then 1 inch more (or desired amount) to wrong side; topstitch. Hang curtain on the rod.

Chair Pad: Cut two pieces of fabric from your pattern. Cut three pieces of batt, omitting the seam allowance. Cut two 1½ × 30-inch ties.

Fold the ties in half lengthwise, wrong side out, and press. Stitch the long edges to make a ¼-inch seam. Use a small safety pin to turn them right side out. Tuck in ends and sew closed.

Fold ties at the center; pin the fold to the right side of one cushion piece at dot with ends of the ties facing in.

With the raw edges matching, pin piping to the right side of the other cushion piece along the seamline, overlapping ends.

With right sides together, the piping and ties sandwiched between, stitch back and front together, using zipper foot and leaving large opening. Insert 3 layers of batting. Sew opening closed.

Checkpoint Pillow

MATERIALS
Fabric, 45-inch-wide blue-background (A) and white-background (B) cotton prints, ⅜ yard each
Pillow form, 25-inch square

Cut 24 A and 26 B 3½-inch squares (includes ¼-inch seam allowance). Alternating colors, stitch squares together in ten rows of five squares each. Press seam allowances to one side. Stitch five rows together for front, five for back. See General Directions to complete a Two-piece Pillow.

RUFFLES IN VIEW

For a narrow window that opens to a less-than-scenic view, tiers of overlapping valances on tension rods provide something good to look at inside. You can buy the valances or run up your own.

MATERIALS
Ready-made valances or fabric (see instructions to estimate amount)
Thin tension rods

Measure window and estimate the number of evenly spaced rods you will need (ruffles should overlap a bit). If using ready-made valances, slide them onto the rods, then push the rod ends against the inside of window frames.

To make ruffles, cut each piece twice as long as the horizontal measurement and 4 inches more than the vertical measurement to allow for hem, top ruffle, and rod pocket. For each ruffle, narrowly hem ends, then press ½ inch under on long edges. Press another inch on lower edge and hem. Fold the top edge under 2 inches and hem; topstitch about ¾ inch above hemline for rod pocket. Insert rods into the pockets and hang the ruffles.

THE PRIDE OF THE PANTRY

s sweet as an old wallpaper-lined French hatbox, this pantry is lined with glazed chintz stapled to walls and shirred on rods in front of cabinet doors. Sewing time for the shirring is a matter of minutes.

Wall Covering

MATERIALS:
Fabric or sheets, enough to cover wall with sheet hems cut away or opened out and pressed
Staple gun
White glue

See Fabric-Covered Walls under General Directions. Remove any molding, then replace or add it after the fabric has been applied.

Cabinet Curtains

MATERIALS
Fabric or sheet, to match walls (see instructions to estimate yardage)
Curtain rods, 2 for each curtain

For each curtain you will need fabric 2½ times as wide as the cabinet area to be covered and 3 inches longer.

Fold 1½ inches under at top and bottom, then topstitch for the rod pockets. Attach the rod fixtures to the top and bottom of the cabinet, gather the curtain on the rods, and hang it on the fixtures.

RETHINKING BISTRO CLOTH

The ubiquitous European and American checkered tablecloth fabric goes into a new mode when fringed 6-inch squares are stitched to white curtain panels to form a giant checkerboard.

Size: Each panel, 21¼ inches wide × 35½" long or length desired; pair fits standard-width (30-inch) window.

MATERIALS

Fabric for one pair of curtains: 1⅛ yards (or 3½ inches more than desired finished length) of 44-inch-wide white lightweight cotton-blend piqué; ⅝ yard (or one half the yardage of piqué) of 54-inch-wide checkered tablecloth fabric

Fabric for six napkins: 1 yard checkered fabric

Cut white fabric 3½ inches longer than desired length, then cut it in half lengthwise or ¾ inch more than the desired width of each panel. Topstitch ¼-inch hem on side selvage edges, ¼-inch finished hem (see General Directions) on side cut edges.

Cut checkered fabric into 6-inch squares. Pin them to the white panels in a checkerboard pattern, as shown, leaving 1¼ inches uncovered at top of the panel and 2¼ inches at bottom for hem; trim as needed to fit at side edge.

Topstitch the squares in place ½ inch in from edges. Pull loose threads to fringe them down to the stitching line.

At curtain top turn ¼ inch under, then 1¼ inches; stitch to make 1 inch for the rod pocket. At lower edge turn ¼ inch under, then 2 inches; hem.

For napkins, cut checkered fabric into 18-inch squares. Stitch ½ inch in from edges. Fringe edges to the stitching line.

PRETTY AIRS FOR THE BATH

o bathroom is too small to be brightened, prettified, and softened with fabric. Opportunities range from the obvious shower and window curtain to the more unexpected sink skirt to a surprising, attractive shirred frame for the medicine-cabinet mirror.

DINGY BATHROOM SOAKS UP COLOR

An unglamorous bathroom "of a certain age" gets a new lease on life with a colorful shower curtain, sink skirt, and chair rail made of sheet fabric. Partner in the brightening—fresh paint.

Shower Curtain

MATERIALS
Sheet, full-size
Shower curtain, clear plastic, for liner
Grommets, same number as in liner
Pole hooks, for grommets

Cut the sheet about 4 inches longer and 3 inches wider than the liner. Topstitch 1-inch hems at sides and bottom, 2-inch at the top. Following instructions with the package, insert grommets in the top hem, spacing them the same as the hook holes on the liner. Hook the liner and curtain to the shower pole.

Sink Skirt

MATERIALS
Sheet, twin-size
Adhesive-backed hook-and-loop tape
    (such as Velcro Sticky Back®), ¾-inch-
    wide, to fit sides and front of sink

Open the top hem on the sheet and press. Cut two pieces the width of the sheet and 3 inches longer than the top-to-floor measurement of the sink. Stitch the pieces together at the sides. Make 3-inch hem at the bottom.

Run gathering stitches ½ inch, ¾ inch, and 1 inch from the top edge. Pull the threads so the skirt fits the sides and front rim of the sink.

For a binding, cut a 3-inch-wide sheeting strip the length of the sink rim; press the raw edges under ½ inch. Fold the strip in half lengthwise, right side out; pin it over the gathered edge of the skirt. Topstitch through all thicknesses close to the edges and ends of the binding.

Follow the directions for the self-stick tape and press one section to the sink rim. Stitch the other section to the back of the binding. Press the sections together.

Chair Rail

MATERIALS
Fabric, leftover sheeting from sink skirt
Molding strip, ¾-inch-wide, to fit top
    and bottom of trim, as shown
Finishing nails, 1-inch
Wood filler
Paint
Brush, small square-tipped
Masking tape

Cut 3½-inch-wide strips of sheeting to go around the wall above the tile or about 36 inches up from the floor. Tape the strips to the wall, stitching them together end to end, or turning the ends under and butting them. Cut the molding to fit the top and bottom edges of the strips. Lap the molding ½ inch over the fabric edges and nail in place, countersinking the nailheads. Fill the holes with wood filler, then paint the molding.

TOWELS ARE A NATURAL

F old eyelet-edged bath towels over a rod, then tie up their fronts with fingertip towels for an ingenious and appropriate window treatment. The valance is a towel cut to fit.

MATERIALS
Lightweight towels, 3 trimmed bath and 2 fringed fingertip (bath towels should be about same width as window)
Eyelet lace, 1½-inch-wide, ½ yard

Curtains
For each curtain panel, lay a bath towel facedown; fold long sides in to meet at the center. Fold the front (trimmed) edge down to about 1 inch longer than the back edge. Adjusting it to desired length, turn the folded end back to form a rod pocket, then tack to close the pocket.

From the center of a fingertip towel cut a 1½-inch-wide strip lengthwise; wrap one of the remaining wider pieces around the front of the curtain panel, crossing the ends as shown. Wrap and tack where they cross with a section cut from the narrow strip, then cover the strip with a piece of eyelet lace.

Valance
Cut the third bath towel in half width-wise and discard one half. For a rod pocket, fold the cut edge of the remaining half toward the finished edge, adjusting the length. Make a rod pocket as before and, using half of the remaining fingertip towel, wrap it around the center, as for the curtains.

CABINET FRAME

Another way to ease the clinical atmosphere of a bathroom is with this frame for the medicine-cabinet mirror: a wood form wrapped with shirred fabric and fastened with tape.

MATERIALS

Fabric, 1½ yards cotton-blend print
Wooden strips, 1½-inch-wide, to fit around mirror
Wood glue
Nails
Quilt batting, strip the length of wooden strips
Staple gun
Adhesive-backed hook-and-loop tape, (such as Velcro Sticky Back®) length of wooden strips

Cut the wooden strips to fit around the mirror, then assemble them with glue and nails. Cut the fabric in strips about 3 inches wide and twice as long as the perimeter of the mirror, piecing them as necessary. Cut the batting to go around the mirror once. Hold the batting against the frame and wrap the fabric around and around it, overlapping the raw edges and gathering and stapling as you go. Cut the tape to fit the frame; stick and staple it around the back of the frame. Press other half of the tape on the mirror, then press the frame to the mirror.

CURTAIN GOING UP

A floor-to-ceiling shower curtain is often a custom job, but just slip the hem of a sheet onto a high rod, and you have it made. Pillowcases to match are used for the simple curtains.

MATERIALS
Sheet, 1 twin-size for standard 5-foot tub
Pillowcases, 2 for curtains
Shower curtain, clear plastic, for liner
Shower curtain hooks
Grommets
Tension rod (optional)

Shower Curtain
Following the manufacturer's directions, attach grommets through the hem on the sheet, using the same spacing as the hook holes in the liner. Insert hooks through the matching holes and hang curtains on an existing shower rod or on a tension rod.

Window Curtains
Stitch pillowcases together on the long edge. Drape curtain over the curtain rod with the seam on the top of the rod. Fold up one corner of the front case as shown and tack or pin.

RUFFLE FOR A WINDOW

A strip of ruffle goes a long way decoratively, held in place around a bathroom window by hooks concealed at the corners. This is such a quick fix that you might even want to make a seasonal wardrobe of window ruffles. Note: This ruffle works well only where the windowsill is flush with the wall.

MATERIALS
Fabric, 1½ yards cotton-blend print
Elastic, ¼-inch-wide and long enough
   to fit perimeter of window frame
Cup hooks, 4
Curtain rings, 4 small

Cut fabric into 10-inch-wide strips. Sew them end to end, making one long strip twice the perimeter of the window frame. Fold the strip in half lengthwise, right side out, and stitch ⅜ inch from the raw edges to form a tube. Turn raw ends in, then press the tube with the seam at center back. Topstitch two lines, ½ inch apart, lengthwise down the middle of the tube from one end to the other.

Screw one cup hook into each corner of the window frame. Run a strip of elastic, stretching it slightly, from hook to hook all the way around the frame, and cut it to this length.

Feed the elastic through the ½-inch channel of the tube (use a closed safety pin to work it through). Sew ends of the elastic together, then sew ends of the tube together.

Test-fit the ruffle around the window frame and mark the location on the ruffle for four rings to match the hooks. Sew on rings and attach the ruffle to the hooks.

HARD-WORKING SINK SKIRT

T he sink skirt is an asset in any bath, especially in a small one. It looks pretty, hides the pipes, and creates a storage space for cleaning aids and extra supplies.

MATERIALS
Fabric, cotton-blend solid-color or print
   (see instructions to estimate yardage)
Adhesive-backed hook-and-loop tape,
   (such as Velcro Sticky Back®), ¾-inch-
   wide

To determine fabric yardage, measure from sink top to floor and add 2 inches. Then measure around three sides of the sink and double the measurement.

Cut the skirt into two pieces for access to storage area under the sink. Top-stitch a 2-inch hem at the lower edge and 1-inch hem at sides. Fold top edge under 1½ inches, then gather it to fit sides and front of the sink.

Fasten the skirt to the sink with self-fastening tape as follows: Press loop strip around three sides of the sink about 2 inches below top edge, then sew hook strip to the wrong side of gathers on the skirt.

SWAGS FOR SOFTNESS

Generous windows are a luxury in a bathroom, but you often have to provide privacy with such means as these matchstick blinds. For a soft note, top the blinds with swag valances.

MATERIALS

Fabric, floral cotton-blend (see Balloon Shades under General Directions to estimate yardage)

Shirring tape, the width of the shade

Roman shade ring tape, the length of the shade for each balloon, plus 1 more length

Pull-cord, 8 times the length of the shade

Wooden strip, 1 × 2 inches × the width of window frame, for mounting board

Screw eyes, 1 for each vertical channel between balloons and 1 for each side edge (the opening must be large enough to accommodate all cords easily, see instructions)

Angle irons, 2

Cleat or ring to fasten pull-cords

Thin metal rod, width of finished shade

Staple gun, with ½-inch staples

Yardstick

To make the valance shade, see Balloon Shades under General Directions. When lowered completely the valance becomes a shade, or, if made shorter, it can be simply a flowery valance.

THE BEDROOM AS MOOD-MAKER

The bedroom is the natural place to display all that fabric has to offer: its coddling qualities and its mood-making punch. Being private—no concerns about impressions made, no inhibitions about your fantasy of who you are or would like to be. This is the all-out self-expression, wish-fulfillment room, so lay on the ruffles, pretend you're a princess, overdose on your favorite frothy color. And don't worry a lot about what your husband will think. Most men get a kick out of being in what is obviously a lady's bedroom.

DELICIOUS VICTORIANA

A Victorian bedroom like this can make you feel as wonderful as wearing a ball gown. Elements to make include vanity skirt, quilt, and ruffled cushions. Floral-print sheets are the fabric throughout.

Comforter

Size: About 84 inches square

MATERIALS

Fabric, 1 flat queen-size sheet and 1 flat king-size floral print sheet with wide border design; 1 flat twin-size sheet in coordinating solid color

Quilt batts, 2 thick queen-size polyester

Threads, white and to match solid-color sheet

White crochet cotton and large-eye sharp needle for tufting (optional)

Carefully open the sheet hems and remove any lace trims. Launder sheets to wash out the sizing.

Following the cutting diagram, and measuring carefully, cut pieces from the queen-size sheet, centering part of the border design on A and B units, another part on E strips. In the same manner, cut pieces from the king-size sheet, cutting four additional 5-inch squares (F) from the most densely patterned part of the border.

Cut the solid-color twin-size sheet lengthwise, beginning at a corner, as follows: two each 3-inch-wide border strips in lengths of 85, 81, 73, 69, 61, and 57 inches. (Label these pairs of strips 1 through 6, from the smallest to the largest.)

Cut twelve solid-color 10⅞-inch squares (C) and four 11⅝-inch squares; cut large squares in half diagonally to form triangles (D).

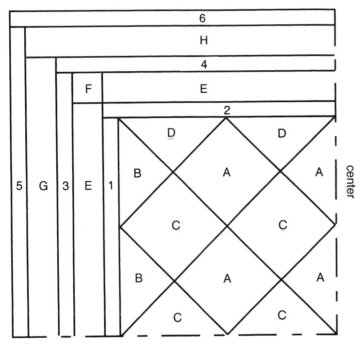

center
Quarter Assembly Diagram

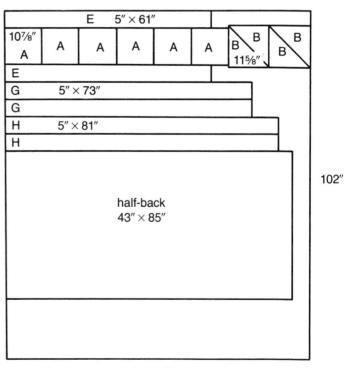

90"
Cutting Diagram for Queen-Size Sheet

From solid-color scraps, cut 2-inch-wide bias strips (see General Directions) and join them to make a 350-inch strip for the binding. Press ½ inch under along each long edge. (Note: A ½-inch seam allowance is included in measurements. Place right sides of fabric together to stitch all seams. Press all seams open.)

Following the Quarter Assembly Diagram, lay out squares A and C and triangles B and D. Matching the square corners, seam the units together in diagonal rows, then join the rows to form a 57-inch square. Stitch the shortest solid-color strips (No. 1 on diagram) to opposite sides of the square, then the next largest strips (No. 2) to remaining sides. Stitch E strips in place, adding an F square to each corner. Continue in order as shown.

Stitch the two half-back pieces together to form an 85-inch square. Cut two 85-inch squares from quilt batts. Spread out the back, wrong side up; place quilt batt on top and cover them with the assembled top, right side up. Keeping edges lined up, pin or baste all layers together from the center out to the corners and sides, then around the outer edges.

Set the sewing machine for thick fabric. Use white thread for bobbin (to match the back) and dark thread for the top to match the dark color. Stitch along seamlines of top through all thicknesses. If desired, tuft corners with the crochet cotton. To do this, thread the large-eye needle with two 6-inch lengths of crochet cotton. At a corner, make a small stitch from right side, to wrong to right, through all fabric thicknesses. Remove the needle, knot the thread ends together, then trim, leaving about ½-inch ends.

With ½-inch seam, stitch one long edge of the bias strip around the outer edge of the comforter, matching outer edges and working mitered corners (see General Directions). Stitch the ends of the bias strip together where they meet. Fold half of the binding over the raw edges to the back of the comforter. Turn the raw edge under ½ inch and slipstitch in place, folding excess fabric under at the corners.

Vanity Skirt

MATERIALS

Fabric, 2 flat king-size sheets to match bedding

Shirring tape, to fit table edge front and sides

Adhesive-backed hook-and-loop tape (such as Velcro Sticky Back®)

Measure the table from top to floor and add 1½ inches. Cut the top section from each sheet to the determined measurement, using the full sheet width. Fold the cut edge (top of skirt) 1½ inches to the wrong side and stitch the shirring tape 1 inch below the fold, over the raw edge. Pull up the shirring threads to fit the side and front of the table edge. Fasten the threads securely.

Following the manufacturer's directions, stick one section of the hook-and-loop tape to the table edge and stitch the other section to the skirt over the shirring tape. Press the sections together.

Seat Pad

MATERIALS

Fabric, enough to cover foam-cushion form and to cover cord for welting (see Bias Strips under General Directions)

Welting cord, twice the measurement around the form

Foam-cushion form, 2-inch-thick, to fit window seat

Cut two rectangles the size of the form, adding ½-inch seam allowance to all edges. Cut a 3-inch-wide boxing strip for each of the four sides of the form, adding ½-inch seam allowance at ends.

Follow General Directions to make corded welting. With raw edges matching, pin the welting to the right side of the top and bottom fabric pieces along the seamlines. Cut the cord so the ends meet, but leave 1 inch of excess fabric to lap and turn under at the ends. Stitch welting along the seamlines.

Alternating the sides and ends, stitch the boxing strips together to form ring.

With right sides facing, the welting sandwiched between, and the seams at the corners, stitch the ring to the top. Stitch the other edge of the ring to the bottom, leaving one end open. Turn the cover right side out, insert the form, and sew the opening closed.

Ruffled Cushion for Sidechair

MATERIALS

Fabrics, ⅝ yard 45-inch-wide cotton-blend floral print for cover top and ruffle; ¼ yard dark solid or coordinating print for welting and ties; ¾ yard white muslin for cover bottom and cushion

Polyester stuffing, for cushion
Cord, 1¼ yards of ¼-inch-diameter, for welting

Measure your chair seat to determine the cushion size and shape (ours is 16 inches wide at front, tapered to 14 inches wide at back, and 15 inches long). Make a paper pattern, adding ½-inch seam allowance all around. Use the pattern to cut one cushion cover top from the print fabric, two cushion pieces from muslin. Cut the paper pattern in half crosswise; cut one muslin piece from each pattern half for the cover bottom, adding 2 inches to crosscut edges (bottom cover has an overlapped center opening). For the ruffle, cut 6-inch-wide strips of floral fabric, joining them as necessary to make a piece twice the length of the measurement around the cushion front and sides. From the dark fabric, cut two strips each 2 × 38 inches for ties, and make one bias strip 2 × 44 inches, piecing as necessary, for welting (see General Directions).

To make the muslin cushion, see Two-piece Pillow under General Directions. Stuff cushion with polyester.

To make corded welting, see General Directions.

Make a ¼-inch hem along one long edge of the ruffle strip. Sew a row of gathering stitches ⅜ inch from the opposite edge and pull up the stitching to fit the cover.

To assemble the cover, see Three-piece Pillow under General Directions.

Fold the tie strips in half lengthwise, right side out; turn in raw edges ¼ inch and topstitch all around. Tack the center of a tie at each back corner of cushion.

Hatboxes

MATERIALS

Fabric, chintz or other decorator fabric
  (see instructions to estimate yardage)
Paint roller, foam covered, 3 inches
  wide
Hatbox
White glue
Large plate and roller, for rolling glue
Paper, for pattern

To make patterns: Measure height and circumference of the box side; add 2½ inches to height and ¾ inch to circumference. Cut a strip of paper the determined size. Place the lid upside down on the paper; trace around the edge and cut out, adding ¾ inch all around. Measure the lid side and add ¾ inch to height and circumference; cut a strip. Cut a paper circle ¼ inch smaller all around than the box bottom.

From your paper patterns you can estimate the amount of fabric you will need, but be sure to determine which direction (vertically or horizontally) you will want to cut the pieces to make the best use of the printed design. Press your fabric and cut the pieces from the patterns.

To cover lid: Lay the larger fabric circle flat on the table, wrong side up. Pour glue onto the plate; push roller back and forth to pick up the glue, then roll it evenly onto the lid top. Place lid, glue side down, on center of fabric. Turn right side up and press fabric onto top. Clip the ¾-inch allowance from the outer edge to lid every half inch. Apply glue to side of lid with the edge of roller. Press the clipped fabric down all around the side edges.

To cover the lid side, press ¼ inch under at top and one end of the fabric strip. Starting with raw end, and placing the folded edge even with top, glue the strip to the lid side. Clip allowance and glue inside the rim.

To cover box: Press ¼ inch under on one end of the strip. Center fabric on the box side and, starting with the raw end of strip, apply glue and attach fabric to a section; turn the box and do next section, ending with the folded end overlapping the raw end. Clip allowances and fold them inside top and over the bottom.

Center and glue the bottom circle to the box, covering the raw edge of the fabric side.

Picture Frame

Size: Oval, 6 × 8 inches, with 3 × 4½-inch opening.

MATERIALS

Fabric, scrap of sheet or other tightly
  woven fabric, ¼ yard
Quilt batting, 6 × 8 inches
Matte boards, four 6 × 8-inch pieces
  (2 each for frame and stand)
Ribbon, 6 inches of ⅝-inch-wide
  grosgrain
White glue
Hot-melt glue gun
Craft knife
Felt-tip marker

On paper draw a pattern for an oval frame 6 × 8 inches with an opening to fit the picture. The frame itself should be about 1½ to 2 inches wide. Using the pattern and craft knife, cut two pieces (front and back) from matte board, then cut a center opening from one piece (front) for the picture. Also cut from the board two rectangles for the stand, half the width and two-thirds the length of the frame back; taper the long sides so the width of each top is half the width of each bottom.

With marker, trace the frame front on quilt batting and on the wrong side of the fabric, making sure to trace the center opening. Cut out batting. Adding a 1-inch allowance along outer and center opening edges, cut fabric for front and back.

Glue the batt lightly to the front board. Center the front fabric, right side up, over the batt. Turn the front over to bring the board side up. Clipping at curves, fold the fabric edges around opening to the back of board and fasten with hot glue. Glue the outer edges in the same manner.

Cut the fabric for one side of each stand, adding ¾ inch all around. Cut the lining for one stand back ⅛ inch smaller all around. Glue fabric to each stand front, gluing edges to back. Cover the back of one stand with the lining fabric.

To hinge the stand, cut a 1½-inch piece of ribbon. Hot-glue ¾ inch of one end to the center top of the unlined back and glue other half of the ribbon to the center top of the lined back. Cut a 4½-inch piece of ribbon. Glue ¾ inch of both ends to the stand pieces, centering ribbon on the inner bottom edges of the stand.

Tape the picture to the back of the frame opening. Attach the frame front to the back with hot glue, a few sewing stitches, or double-faced tape. Centering the stand on the back of the frame with bottom edges flush, glue the uncovered side of the stand to the back of the frame.

LACE BUTTERFLY AT THE WINDOW

The luxury of lace and the ease of no-sew installation are the benefits of this unusual window design, one that you can adapt to almost any window and almost any piece of lace.

MATERIALS
Tablecloth, to fit window
Curtain rings, about 3
Cup hooks, same number as rings

To achieve our arrangement, sew a ring to the center of your cloth, then two more rings near diagonally opposite corners. Screw a cup hook to the top center of the window frame and one to each upper corner. Hang the rings on the hooks, draping the cloth as shown.

FRANKLY FROU-FROU

Perfect for a lace valentine lady are curtains made of lavender bridal tulle trimmed with satin zigzag edges and wreathed at the top with silk flowers.

MATERIALS
Fabric, fine tulle (see instructions to estimate yardage)
Satin ribbon, ⅝-inch-wide
Artificial flowers

To estimate fabric yardage, measure from rod to floor for the desired length and add 10 inches for the heading and casing. The width of each curtain panel should be the full width of the window. Sew lengths of tulle together for the desired width.

Starting at the top, cut center edges of tulle straight for 10 inches, then cut sawtooth edges. Topstitch ribbon along these edges, mitering corners (see General Directions).

Fold top down 10 inches. To form heading and rod casing, topstitch 7 inches and 9 inches from the fold. Tack flowers to the heading. Tiebacks are flower-trimmed ribbons.

IS THERE A PRINCESS IN THE HOUSE?

The crown canopy is a variation on the ready-made curtains at the window and it sets the tone in this regal bedroom, which also stars a padded headboard, tiered dressing-table and stool skirts, upholstered mirror frame, and ribbon-tied lampshade covers.

Canopy

MATERIALS

Printed priscilla curtains, 2 pairs, for canopy

Fabric or sheet, plain, to gather behind headboard (see instructions to estimate yardage)

Pine half circle, 1-inch-thick, 24-inch-diameter, for crown

Fabric glue

Nails, to fasten crown to ceiling

Cleats or rings, 2, to fasten tiebacks

Cut the ruffle from the top of one pair of curtains; cut the curved bottom of the second pair straight across. Stitch the cut top edge of the first pair to the cut bottom of the second pair to make one long pair.

For the back piece, cut the fabric the same length as the curtains and twice as wide as the headboard, piecing if necessary. Hem the lower and side edges. Gather and staple the raw top edge across the straight edge of the wooden crown.

Nail the crown to the ceiling with the straight edge against the wall, sandwiching the gathered edge of the back piece between crown and wall. Cut a half circle of fabric to fit the bottom of the crown, adding 1 inch all around. Glue the 1-inch excess around the

edges of the crown, tucking it between the back piece and the crown.

Fit a curtain ruffle around the curved edge of the crown and staple it, hiding the staples in the folds of fabric.

Fasten the tiebacks to cleats or rings attached to the wall.

Headboard

MATERIALS
Wooden headboard
Fabric or sheet, plain, to fit front and
    back of headboard
Quilt batting, to fit front of headboard
Staple gun
White glue

Cut the batting to the shape of the headboard, then glue it sparingly to the headboard front.

Cut the fabric to fit over the front of the board and wrap it at least 3 inches onto the back. With a helper, stretch the fabric tightly over the batting and staple it to the back of the board, pleating it neatly at curves.

Cut fabric to fit the back of the board, adding 1 inch on all edges. Turn the 1-inch excess under and topstitch. Glue the fabric on the board back (apply the glue to the hem only), making sure the staples are covered.

Lampshade Cover

MATERIALS
Fabric or sheet, to match canopy or
    headboard (see instructions to esti-
    mate yardage)
Ribbon, 1 yard ½-inch-wide

Cut a fabric strip 12 inches wide (or 2 inches wider than shade depth) × 67 inches, piecing if necessary. Stitch the ends together to form a ring. Turn both edges under 1 inch and topstitch. Gather one edge to fit the shade top. Rest the cover over the shade and tie it with ribbon.

Dressing Table and Stool

MATERIALS
Fabrics or sheets, to match canopy and
    headboard (see instructions to esti-
    mate yardage)
Two-string shirring tape, 2½ times
    measurement around stool and
    3 sides of table
Quilt batting, to pad stool top
    (optional)

Dressing table: Cut ruffle strips 2½ times the measurement across the front and two sides of the table, cutting the strips to the following depths: 3 inches more than top-to-floor measurement from one fabric, half that measurement from the second fabric. (Note: We used the scalloped edge of a sheet for the top ruffle.) Hem ends and lower edge if necessary.

Hold the two layers together, top raw edges matching and the narrower piece on top. Turn the top edge under 2 inches and baste. Stitch the shirring tape on wrong side 1 inch below the top edge. Pull the strings, gathering the flounce to fit three sides of the table. Tack the flounce around the table.

Stool: If you are using batting, cut it

to fit the top of the stool. Cut the plain fabric 2 inches larger on all sides. Stretch the fabric over the padded top and staple it to the sides of the stool. Make a flounce in the same manner as for the Dressing Table, but to fit completely around the stool.

Mirror

MATERIALS
Mirror with wooden frame
Fabric or sheet, to match canopy
Quilt batting, to fit frame front
Staple gun
White glue

Remove the mirror from the frame. Cut batting strips to fit the frame front but do not overlap the corners. Glue the strips sparingly to the frame.

Cut four strips of fabric, overlapping at corners, to cover the frame front and wrap about 2 inches to the back. Lay the strips over the frame, wrong side up. Pin mitered corners (see General Directions); stitch and cut away the excess. Stretch the fabric frame right side up over the batting and staple it to the wrong side of the frame at the outer edges and the edges of the opening. Replace the mirror.

GLORIOUS GALLICISM

The pretty and evocative French style depends upon the use of their traditional small prints, which, more and more, are turning up in sheet patterns. Here they cover walls and make festoon blinds, seat pads, and flanged pillows.

Shirred Sheets on Walls

MATERIALS
Sheets, flat (see instructions to estimate yardage)
Thin curtain rods, the number that will fit twice, end to end, across the wall
Cup hooks, 2 for each rod

Place the curtain rods, end to end, on the cup hooks that have been screwed into the wall 1 inch below the ceiling and 1 inch above the floor (turn the floor hooks downward).

From the sheets, cut each panel 2½ times the width of each rod and 5 inches longer than the measurement between top and bottom rods. Top-stitch a 2-inch-wide rod pocket at top and bottom of the panels.

Hang the panels, hooking the bottom rods under the hooks (make slits in the hems for hooks if necessary).

Balloon Shades

MATERIALS
Sheets, flat (see Balloon Shades under General Directions to estimate yardage)
Shirring tape, the width of the shade
Roman shade ring tape, the length of the shade for each balloon, plus 1 more length
Wooden strip, 1 × 2 inches, the width of window frame, for mounting board

Pull-cord, 8 times the length of the
    shade
Screw eyes, 1 for each vertical channel
    between balloons and 1 for each side
    edge (screw-eye opening must be
    large enough to accommodate all
    cords—see instructions)
Angle irons, 2
Awning cleat, 1
Thin metal rod, width of finished
    shade
Staple gun
Yardstick

To make the shade, see Balloon Shades
under General Directions.

Flanged Pillow

MATERIALS
Fabric or sheet, 23 × 46-inch piece for
    cover front and back
Contrasting border, 11 × 108-inch strip
    (piece if necessary)
Pillow form, 22-inch, muslin-covered

Cut two 23-inch squares from fabric or
sheet for the front and back. Stitch the
ends of the border strip together to
form a ring. Press the border in half
lengthwise, right side out. With raw
edges matching, pin the strip to the
right side of the front square, gathering
it at the corners. To assemble the
pillow, see Two-piece Pillow under
General Directions.

Lace-on-Cotton Tablecloth

MATERIALS
Fabric, cotton-blend, 43½-inch square
Lace, 6½ yards 2½-inch-wide, 7¾ yards
    1¼-inch-wide

On the fabric square, baste an X from
corner to corner for guidelines. Mark a
series of six concentric squares, measuring on the lines 2¾ inches, 5¾
inches, 11¼ inches, 14¼ inches, 24
inches, and 27¼ inches from the center.
Using the 2¼-inch-wide lace at the first
set of marks, form a solid square (it fills
the center of the cloth), mitering the
corners (see General Directions). Topstitch along all the lace edges and
mitered corners.

With the 1¼-inch-wide lace, form an
open-square band to fit around the
next set of marks; topstitch it in place.
Alternating narrow and wide laces,
topstitch square bands to the cloth,
then topstitch a ¼-inch hem.

Lace-on-Cotton Pillows (one)

MATERIALS
Fabric, cotton-blend, 1½ yards for cover
    front, back, and ruffle
Lace, 2¾ yards 2½-inch-wide, 3¼ yards
    1¼-inch-wide, 6 yards ½-inch-wide
Pillow form, 24-inch, muslin-covered

From fabric, cut one 25-inch square for
the front, two 14½ × 25-inch for an
overlapped back, and a 3½ × 208-inch
strip for the ruffle (piecing as necessary). Apply the two wider laces to the
pillow front in the same manner as for
the Tablecloth, ending with the 14¼-
inch marks.

With right sides facing and allowing
¼ inch for seam, stitch the ½-inch-wide
lace to the ruffle strip with the lace
heading matching the raw fabric edge.
Press the lace outward and topstitch
close to the seamline. Stitch the ends of
the ruffle together. Gather the raw edge
to fit around the front square; pin to
the front with raw edges matching.

To complete the pillow, see Two-
piece Pillow under General Directions.

SHADY MAGIC

A deep lace border glued to the bottom of a window shade of the same color is a quick shot of luxury for a room. Lace panels, hung from the ceiling, screen off a special corner.

MATERIALS
Lace border, desired width and 1 inch
  longer than width of shade
Window shade
White glue

Narrowly hem the ends of the lace border. If lace has a finished top edge, glue it neatly to the front of the lower edge of the shade. If top edge of lace is a cut edge, simply glue it to the back of the shade.

FEAST OF FLOWERS

Except for the glamorous gauze canopy draped on a holdback, every element of this room is fabulously floral: a bevy of pillows, a bordered blanket, a painted trunk, and a painted sisal rug.

Flowery Pillows

Note: The following pillows and the border for the blanket were all cut from a full-size sheet. However, should you want to make only one pillow, we specify the number of pillowcases you will need.

All pillows require pillow forms, fabric-covered in sizes specified.

If using pillowcases, cut them open at seams and press out.

Chair Pillow
Size: 24-inch diameter

MATERIALS
Floral pillowcases, 2 standard
Glazed cotton, ½ yard 45-inch-wide solid-color

From sheet or pillowcases, cut two 25-inch-diameter circles. Make a glazed-cotton bias strip 3 inches wide to fit around pillow for welting (see General Directions). Press it in half lengthwise, right side out. With raw edges matching, pin the welting to the right side of a circle. See General Directions to complete a Two-piece Pillow.

Neckroll Pillow
Size: 6-inch diameter × 14-inch length

MATERIALS
Pillowcase, 1 standard
Cotton fabric, 6 × 12 inches, solid-color

Eyelet ruffle, 1⅛ yards 2-inch-wide
Satin ribbon, 1¼ yards, ¾-inch-wide

From sheet or pillowcase, cut one 15 × 20-inch rectangle for the center section and two 4 × 20-inch-strips for the ends.

From solid-color fabric, cut two 6-inch-diameter circles.

Hand-sew a circle to each end of the pillow form (there is no need to turn the ends under).

Cut ruffle into two 20-inch lengths. Folding lengths wrong side out, stitch the short ends together (½-inch seam allowance) to form two rings. Repeat with the end strips. Repeat with the center section of the pillow cover to form a tube. Trim the seams on the ruffle rings.

Matching raw edges and seams, pin a ruffle ring to the right side of one end of the center tube. With right sides facing and the ruffle sandwiched between, stitch an end ring to tube end. Repeat at the other end of the tube. Turn right side out.

Turn the edges of end rings under ¼ inch, then ¾ inch; topstitch to form casings. Open the seams about ½ inch on right side of the casing to insert ribbon. Cut ribbon in half and thread each half through a casing. Slide the cover over the pillow form, pull up ribbons and tie in bows.

Appliquéd Square Pillow
Size: 18-inch square

MATERIALS
Large-motif floral pillowcase, 1 standard

Glazed cotton, ⅝ yard solid-color
Welting cord, 2¼ yards

Cut out two 19-inch squares from glazed cotton. From sheet or pillowcase, roughly cut out three or four floral motifs for appliqué. See General Directions to make Bias Strips and Corded Welting from remainder.

Trim the appliqués neatly; pin them to one cotton square at least ½ inch in from edges. Work close machine-zigzag stitch over edges of the appliqués.

See General Directions to complete a Two-piece Pillow.

Eyelet-ruffled Round Pillow
Size: 14-inch diameter

MATERIALS
Floral pillowcase, 1 standard
Eyelet ruffle, 1⅜ yards 3-inch-wide

Cut out two 15-inch-diameter circles from sheet or pillowcase. Cut ruffle to the circumference of the circle plus 1 inch, then stitch the ends together (½-inch seam allowance), and trim.

With raw edges matching, pin ruffle to right side of a circle; topstitch.

See General Directions to complete a Two-piece Pillow.

Appliquéd Round Pillow
Size: 19-inch diameter

MATERIALS
Large-motif floral pillowcases,
  2 standard
Glazed cotton, ⅝ yard solid-color

Cut out two 20-inch-diameter circles from glazed cotton.

Roughly cut a floral motif for appliqué from sheet or pillowcase. From sheet or other pillowcase, cut 5-inch-wide strips for pleating; piece them to measure 195 inches.

Trim the appliqué neatly; pin it to the center of one circle. Work close-matching zigzag stitch over the edges.

Topstitch ¼-inch finished hem on one long edge of the pleating strip. Mark 2-inch intervals on the long raw edge of the strip. Working on an ironing board, fold a ¾-inch-deep pleat to left at each mark, pinning and pressing pleats as you go. Test-fit the strip around the pillow top and adjust first and last pleats to match others, allowing ½ inch for seam. Stitch the ends of the strip to form a ring. With raw edges matching, pin the ring to the right side of the appliquéd circle; topstitch.

See General Directions to complete a Two-piece Pillow.

Canopy

MATERIALS
Chiffon or gauze (see instructions to estimate yardage)
Drapery holdback with 2 extensions to make longer
Hardware specified for holdback
Ball of string

Attach extensions to the holdback, making it about 9 inches long. Fasten it to the wall about 7 feet above the floor. To estimate fabric needed, drape string over the holdback. Measure the string and buy the length of fabric indicated; drape it over the holdback.

PERFECT COORDINATION READY-MADE

Here is one way to use readymades for a charming and harmonious bedroom. Start with curtains and coordinating bed skirts (one extra). Use the extra bed skirt, with a little refitting, on a big dressing table, and then top it with a coordinating coverlet.

MATERIALS
Quilted bed coverlet with ruffle
Dust ruffle with mattress cover
Curtains, to coordinate with coverlet
   and dust ruffle
Staple gun or tacks
Rectangular table
Glass top cut to fit tabletop

Arrange the dust ruffle around the table edge with its lower edge at floor level. Trim away excess mattress cover, leaving enough to staple or tack all around the edge of the tabletop; hem cut edge if desired. Staple or tack the skirt to the table so that the ends meet at center back; cut away any excess ruffle at the back.

Place the coverlet over the table as shown. If too large, remove its trim and ruffle; then cut the coverlet to desired size (with the ruffle, it should cover the top of the dust ruffle). Reattach the trim and ruffle, cutting away the excess. Place the cover on the table and add the glass top.

PRISCILLA POWER

For a quick custom effect, you can take two pairs of ready-made priscilla curtains in a pretty print, hang one the usual way, and make a valance out of the other. Rosette is easy to form.

MATERIALS
Priscillas (ruffled curtains with attached ruffled valance), 2 pairs
Cord or flexible wire
Hooks or curtain tiebacks, 2
Pushpins

Hang one pair of the curtains. Attach a safety pin to the end of one length of cord (or bend and tape an end of the wire) and draw cord (or wire) through the rod pocket at the top of both panels of the second pair of curtains. Gather fabric as tightly as possible to form a rosette, then fasten ends of cord or wire together.

Attach hooks or tiebacks to each top corner of the window frame. Fasten the rosette at center top with pushpins or cord. Drape the curtains to each side to form a valance, catching the fabric in the corner hooks.

HANKY-PANKY

C an anything this cloud-soft and lacy be accomplished on a budget? Yes, because the elements making up the coverlet, table skirt, and valance are handkerchiefs color-tinted and assembled with lace-topped seams.

Tips on Dyeing Fabric: Use cotton or cotton-blend fabrics, including extra pieces of the same material, for testing colors. Men's handkerchiefs, used for the valance and bedspread, can often be found packaged in variety stores. Wash out any sizing. Have ready a pair of rubber gloves; a long metal spoon for stirring; a stainless steel, enamel, or glass container for wet fabrics; a clothesline; and newspapers.

Follow the dye manufacturer's directions for sink dyeing. The color you'll get depends on the strength of the dye bath, the type of fabric, and the length of time immersed. Make test swatches and label them with color name, dyeing time, and the proportion of dye to water. Rinse dyed pieces in cold water immediately, wring them out thoroughly, and hang to dry to prevent streaking. Place newspapers on the floor under drying items to prevent stains. Pieces that dry too light can be immersed again. Colors shown include pale blue (PB), light blue (LB), and blue (B); light pink (LP) and rose (R).

MATERIALS
Handkerchiefs, men's (about 16-inch square) for bedspread and valance, women's lace-edged (about 11-inch square) for tablecloth (see instruc-

Bedspread

top

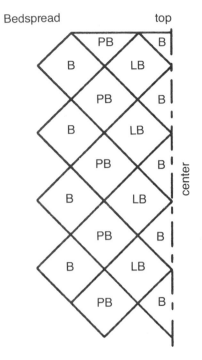

	PB	B
B	LB	
	PB	B
B	LB	
	PB	B
B	LB	
	PB	B
B	LB	
	PB	B

center

Tablecloth

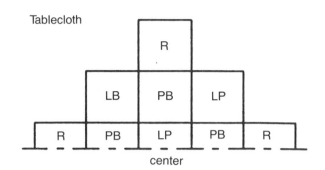

		R		
	LB	PB	LP	
R	PB	LP	PB	R

center

Valance

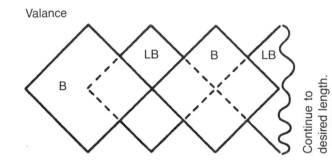

| B | LB | B | LB |

Continue to desired length.

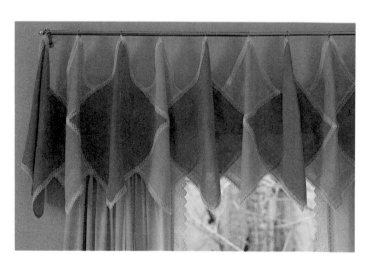

126

tions for quantity or to estimate quantity)
Lace, 1-inch-wide, to cover seams and edges on bedspread and valance
Dye, desired colors (see Tips on Dyeing Fabric)

Bedspread

You will need thirty handkerchiefs for a twin- or full-size bed, thirty-eight for a queen- or king-size bed.

Following the Bedspread Diagram, lap the edges of handkerchiefs ¼ inch; pin and topstitch. Cut and hem top edge with ½-inch finished hem (see General Directions). Topstitch or zig-zag-stitch lace over the seams and edges, mitering corners (see General Directions) at edge of the spread.

Valance

Refer to the Valance Diagram. You will need a strip of handkerchiefs about twice the width of window (Note: A 16-inch-square handkerchief measures about 22½ inches on the diagonal).

Lap the handkerchiefs as shown; topstitch, then topstitch or zigzag stitch lace over the edges of the overlying squares, mitering the corners. Stitch lace to the exposed corners of underlying squares.

Tablecloth

Refer to the Tablecloth Diagram. You will need thirteen handkerchiefs to make a cloth about 53 inches wide. For a larger cloth, add handkerchiefs in the same manner to reach desired size.

Lap the edges of handkerchiefs, adjusting the depth of lap to the smallest and placing all lace edges on top; topstitch.

BOTANICAL BEDROOM

Framed within an easy-to-make alcove canopy stands a bed dressed up in the same botanical sheets; one pillowcase is hung as a picture. Your finishing touch: ribbon trimming on pillowcases and bed skirt.

Dust Ruffle and Shams

MATERIALS
Dust ruffle, solid-color
Pillow shams, floral (to match other bedding)
Grosgrain ribbon, ⅝-inch-wide, measurement of sham ruffles and twice measurement of dust ruffle

Baste two lengths of ribbon, about 1 inch apart, along the edge of the dust ruffle and one length along the edge of each sham ruffle, turning ends under. Topstitch both edges of ribbons.

Canopy

MATERIALS
Sheets, 1 king- and 2 twin-size flat for canopy, to fit full- or queen-size bed
Tree branches, 4 about 1½-inch-diameter (2 about 6 inches longer than width of bed and 2 about 18 inches long)
Grosgrain ribbon, ⅝-inch-wide, 28 yards to trim canopy, and make ties
Nylon monofilament
Screw eyes, 4 large with 1½-inch holes
Nails, 2-inch

For back section of the canopy, cut and hem the king-size sheet the same length as twin sheets (side sections). Fold the twin sheets in half lengthwise,

right side out. Lap edges 1 inch over sides of the back section; topstitch.

Fold ribbon over the upper and folded edges of the drapery. Baste, then topstitch the ribbon.

Cut remaining ribbon into 24-inch lengths. Fold each length in half crosswise. Starting and ending at the two top corners, stitch the fold of each ribbon securely to the top of the drapery, spacing folds evenly.

For the canopy frame, cross the ends of the longer branches over the ends of the shorter branches to form a rectangle, letting 3 inches extend beyond crossings; nail them together to secure, then wind them tightly with the nylon monofilament.

With a helper, lift the frame over the bed and against the wall. Mark the placement of screw eyes on the ceiling to correspond to the corner crossings of the frame. Insert a screw eye at each mark. Attach the frame to the ceiling with the monofilament threaded through the screw eyes and around the frame corners.

To hang the drapery, knot ribbons over the frame, letting ends hang down as shown.

Picture

MATERIALS
Pillow sham, floral, to match bedding
Picture frame, to fit motif on sham
Foam core (available at art stores), to fit inside frame
Masking tape
Staple gun

Cut a rectangular floral motif from the sham, leaving at least 2 inches extra all around. Wrap the edges neatly around the foam core, taping fabric on back to hold it taut. Secure with staples; insert motif in the frame.

COZY COCOON OF FLANNEL SHEETS

For a bedroom that is like a warm hug, you can start by covering the walls with fluffy brushed-flannel sheets. More of the sheets make curtains, table skirt, and duvet. Naturally the bed is made up with matching sheets.

All items shown were made from brushed-flannel flat sheets. See General Directions for sheet sizes.

Flannel Walls

Note: This is not practical for a wall over 8 feet high.

MATERIALS

Sheets, enough to cover wall, with hems cut away or opened and pressed; 1¼-inch-wide strips cut from sheets, long enough to fit around ceiling molding and floor molding
Staple gun
White glue

See Fabric-Covered Walls under General Directions, bringing the fabric to top and bottom moldings. Do not remove the moldings.

To cover the staples, fold edges of the sheet strips under ¼ inch and press. Glue the strips over the row of staples at floor and ceiling moldings.

Round Table Skirt

MATERIALS

Printed sheet, to fit over table to floor, plus 2 inches for hem
White muslin sheet, same size, for liner
Eyelet ruffling, 4-inch-wide, to fit around printed sheet 8 inches from cut edge
Piping to match color in printed sheet, same yardage as ruffling

See Circular Tablecloth under General Directions. Cut a cloth from the printed

sheet and another from the white sheet for liner.

Topstitch a 2-inch hem on the printed skirt, a 3-inch hem on the liner, clipping and overlapping the allowance so it will lie flat.

Mark a stitching line for the ruffle on the printed skirt 6 inches from the edge.

With the raw edges of the piping matching the ruffle heading, stitch the piping to the right side of the ruffle. Turn the piping up and pin it to the pencil line on the skirt; topstitch. Place the liner on the table, then the printed skirt over it.

Duvet

MATERIALS

Quilt, to be covered

Printed sheets, 2, at least 1½ inches larger on each side than quilt

Eyelet ruffling, 4-inch-wide, to fit around quilt cover

Piping, to match a color in printed sheet, same yardage as ruffling

Snap tape, 6 inches shorter than quilt width

For front and back of the cover, cut sheets 1½ inches larger on each side than your quilt.

Stitch the piping to the ruffle (see Round Table Skirt instructions), but do not fold the piping upward. With raw edges matching, pin the ruffle, piping side down, to the right side of the top sheet, easing around the corners so the ruffle will not cup.

With right sides facing, the ruffle sandwiched between, pin the sheets together. Mark a 6-inch hand opening

near each bottom corner (to pull quilt into the cover) and an opening for the snap tape, which will be centered across the top. Stitch the sheets together, leaving the marked areas open. Remove the pins.

Topstitch the snap tape to the folded seam allowance at the top opening. Hem the hand openings. Turn the cover right side out. Push the quilt into the cover as far as you can, then reach into the hand openings and pull it the rest of the way.

Balloon Shade

MATERIALS

Printed sheets (see Balloon Shades under General Directions to estimate number needed)

Eyelet ruffling, 4-inch-wide, to fit edge of shade

4-string shirring tape, the width of shade

Roman shade ring tape, 4 times the length of a 3-balloon shade (as shown), or 1 length for each balloon plus 1 more length

Pull-cord, 8 times the length of shade

Wooden strip, 1 × 2 inches, the width of the window frame, for mounting board

Screw eyes, 1 for each vertical channel between balloons and 1 for each side edge (the opening must be large enough to accommodate all cords easily—see instructions)

Angle irons, 2

Staple gun, with ½-inch staples

Cleat or ring, to fasten pull-cords

Thin metal rod, width of shade, for shade weight

Yardstick

To make the shade, see Balloon Shades under General Directions, adding ruffling as follows: Cut the sheets for the shade as specified, then, with ruffle heading matching the lower edge of the right side of the shade, stitch with ½-inch seam allowance.

FOUR-WAY WINDOW TREATMENT

hy stop at a valance and side panels, especially if there is something below the window that you want to conceal, like an air conditioner? An under-window curtain can be the "footing" that echoes the heading.

MATERIALS
Draperies (rod-to-floor), with narrow
  valance, 2 pairs
Curtain rods, 2

Hang one pair of draperies and valance over the window. Attach the other rod at sill level and hang the second pair, temporarily, to determine the length. Mark the length, remove the draperies and cut off excess, allowing for a hem the same depth as the hems on the window panels. Hem the panels and rehang them, with valance, under the window.

A QUILT CAN WARM MORE THAN A BED

A Roman shade made from a sturdy quilt (not a fragile antique, of course) is a great anti-shiver tactic for a window over a bed. In the dropped position, the shade has a cozy headboard effect.

MATERIALS

Quilt, at least 2 inches wider than window and long enough to pleat as shown

Sheet or similar fabric, for lining (allow 2¾ inches extra length for each rod pocket)

Plastic curtain rings, 2 for each pocket

Screw eyes, 3

Venetian-blind cord

Laths, ¾ × ¼-inch-wide, cut 1 inch shorter than quilt width, 1 for each rod pocket

Mounting board, 1 × 2 inches, cut to quilt width

Angle irons, three 2 × 2 inches

Cleat or ring, for fastening cords

Staple gun

First, determine the number of pleats you want, marking their placement on the back of the quilt. Then cut the lining sheet or fabric to fit the quilt, adding ½ inch at sides, top, and bottom for hems, plus 2¾ inches to length for each pleat pocket.

Turn all lining edges under ½ inch and press. Spread the lining on the back of the quilt and pin a horizontal pocket in the lining *only* at each pleat marker (be sure a lath slides easily into each pocket). Stitch the pockets. Sew all edges of the lining to the quilt back, leaving pocket ends open. Stitch the lining to the quilt along each pocket stitching.

Using angle irons, fasten the mounting board at top of the window with 1-inch edge flush against the frame.

Sew a plastic curtain ring about 4 inches in from each end of each pocket. Insert three screw eyes in the bottom of mounting board: one 3 inches from one end of the board, the other two aligned with the two rows of curtain rings. Staple the quilt to the front of the mounting board.

Attach the cleat to the side of the window frame nearest the two screw eyes; knot one end of cord to the bottom ring on the same side. Thread the cord up through a row of rings and through both screw eyes. Let the cord hang along one side of the window and cut it about 6 inches below cleat. Knot and thread the remaining cord up through the other row of rings, through the empty screw eye at top, and across through other two screw eyes holding the first cord; cut to the same length as first cord. Pull all the cords and wrap them around the cleat to fasten them.

TERRITORIAL GAIN

Turn a corner into much needed closet space by curtaining it off from ceiling to floor. The valance all around the room makes the corner blend in (you might even do two corners) and stands in for moldings.

Size: Triangular closet, about 53 inches across front

Corner Closet

MATERIALS
Sheets, 3 twin-size
Bias tape, contrasting color, 3 packages ½-inch-wide
Pine strip, ¹⁵⁄₁₆-inch square × 53 inches, to support curtain rod
Lattice, ¼ × 1⅛ × 55 inches, to support valance
Curtain rod
Hollow-wall anchors, nails, or screws for solid walls
Staple gun

Miter the ends of the square pine strip and the valance lattice-support strip (faceup) 45° to fit corner walls, keeping strips full-length.

Cut off the wide hems of two sheets. Fold the raw edge under ¼ inch, then fold enough to enclose the curtain rod loosely; topstitch to form a rod pocket.

Measure the length of the completed curtains. Fasten the ends. Fasten the ends of the square pine strip to the wall across the corner at the appropriate height for the curtains to hang to floor, inserting fasteners at an angle through the wood. Attach the rod to the front with the ends as close to the walls as possible. Hang curtains.

For the valance over the closet, cut a 17¾ × 93-inch strip from third sheet. Fold tape over one long edge; topstitch.

Topstitch finished hem (see General Directions) at ends of strip. On the raw long edge, press ½ inch under, then 1¼ inches for heading; topstitch along first pressed edge.

To make pleats, measure 5 inches along heading; pin next 6 inches into three 1-inch pleats (see diagram); measure 9 inches along the heading; pleat next 6 inches. Continue to pleat every 9 inches. Following the diagram, stitch bottom and inner edge of pleats to hold them in place.

To make attaching strip (flange), cut 1¼-inch fabric strip the same length as the back of the pleated heading. With right side of fabric facing you, lap ¼ inch of the heading over the long edge of the flange; topstitch ⅛ inch below the top of the heading, skipping the pleats. Staple the flange over the top face of the lattice strip so that the valance hangs down over the front edge. Trim the flange to avoid screws. Attach wood to the ceiling over the closet, with the flange pushed against the ceiling.

Room Valance

MATERIALS

Sheets (see instructions to estimate number needed)

Bias tape, contrasting color, ½-inch-wide, enough to fit edge of valance

Lattice, ¼ × 1⅛ inches, to fit around perimeter of room

Hollow-wall anchors, nails, or screws for solid walls

To estimate the amount of sheeting, you will need to cut 19-inch-wide strips pieced to length. For length, measure the perimeter of your ceiling in inches. Divide the number by nine and multiply the result by six; add this to the perimeter figure; then add ½ inch for each seam.

Piece the fabric strips and pleat them, as for the valance over the closet, to fit around the room. Place the lattice strips on the floor around the perimeter of the room. Staple the flange of the valance to top of the lattice; trim. Attach the lattice to the ceiling so that the fabric hangs down in front.

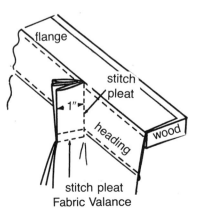

stitch pleat
Fabric Valance

SETTINGS FOR THE YOUNG SET

Loving care for kids combines with a concern for practicality in the bright young playroom/ bedrooms designed for preteens. As for those who have achieved teenhood: she may be a computer whiz or a serious jock but want a bedroom along fairy-tale lines; all want places where they can repair with their friends.

N
othing is crisper than a stripe, and for an extra fillip in this colorful nursery the simple tieback curtains wear a scalloped valance that evokes fairy-tale castles and toy soldiers.

MATERIALS
Fabric, for pair of curtains, tiebacks, and valance (see instructions to estimate yardage)
Bias tape, ¼-inch-wide double-fold, to encircle each valance scallop and tieback
Curtain rod
Valance rod

For each pair of curtains, you will need fabric twice the width of the window (including the frame) and the height of the window plus 6 inches. For a pair of tiebacks, you will need four 4 × 14-inch fabric strips. For the valance, divide the width of the window frame by twelve to determine the width of each scallop. You will need two fabric rectangles the width of each scallop and 10 inches long.

Curtains
Narrowly hem the long edges of each curtain. Turn upper edges under ¼ inch, then 1¾ inches; topstitch to form a casing. Turn up the lower edges ¼ inch, then 3¾ inches; topstitch for hem. Hang on curtain rod.

Tiebacks
Pin pairs of rectangles together right sides out; cut rounded corners. Encase the raw edges with tape; topstitch. Fold tiebacks over the curtain and staple or tack ends to window frame.

Valance
The valance is a series of 12 separate scallops hung on a valance rod. Make each scallop as for the tieback, then fold each in half crosswise and stitch the rounded ends together. Slide them onto the valance rod.

HAPPINESS IS A CRAYON-COLORED CURTAIN

Every child is an artist, at least to begin with, and any child would feel special in a room with muslin curtains and pillows he or she has decorated with iron-on crayons.

MATERIALS

Unbleached muslin, 2½ yards 45-inch-wide (make 1 pair 28-inch-long curtains, valance, and 2 pillows)

Children's wax crayons

Dressmaker's carbon paper (optional)

Tracing paper (optional)

Paper towels

Newspapers

Pillow forms, 2 muslin-covered 14-inch square

Curtain rods, 2

Tips on Drawing Designs: See individual directions to cut muslin. Enlarge the curtain patterns (see General Directions) on tracing paper, or pencil your own or your children's designs. Transfer the patterns to muslin with light-colored dressmaker's carbon. For geometric designs on the valance and pillows, follow the photographs and draw 4-inch squares (overlapped at corners) on the valance and 3-inch-diameter circles on the pillows.

Fill the designs in heavily with crayons, following the photographs, if desired. Use crayons a shade darker than you want (for instance, for a bright yellow, try using an orange-yellow crayon).

FRAMING THE FRAMES

Balloon shades, always charming and practical, are set off in a new way in a little girl's room: the same welting on the shades frames the window casing and is finished with jaunty bows.

MATERIALS
Balloon shade(s)
Thick, round upholstery cord, print-covered (see instructions to estimate yardage)
White glue
Brads

To estimate the amount of cord you will need, measure across the tops of your shades and completely around the outer edges of the window frame. For bows at corners, as shown, you will need about 1½ yards for each bow.

For borders, glue the cord in place, pressing it down well. Tack it here and there, if necessary, to hold more securely. Cut the remaining cord into 1½-yard lengths, tie into bows, and tack to the corners of the window frames.

RUFFLES, FLOURISHES, AND FRAMES

**A**ny old table that doesn't wobble can wear this flouncy tiered slip-on cover. For a preteen or teen the best fun would be an assortment of fabrics, whose leftovers make a group of padded picture frames.

Table Cover

MATERIALS
Fabrics, 1 twin-size plain sheet or 45-inch-wide muslin for tabletop and under-skirt and 5 coordinated prints for ruffles (see instructions to estimate yardages)

Cover can be adapted to fit any table; ours is 19½ inches × 23 inches × 27 inches high.

To estimate fabric amounts, determine the muslin yardage by measuring the tabletop width and the distance from top to floor around the table. For the width of each print ruffle, divide top-to-floor measurement by five and add 2 inches for hems and overlap; for length, double the measurement around the table.

To make a cover for the tabletop, cut sheet of muslin 1 inch larger all around than the top. For under-skirt, cut a piece 1 inch wider than top-to-floor measurement and 1 inch longer than the measurement around the table; stitch the short ends together to form a tube. Stitch the top of tube to the muslin top piece, right sides facing. Turn right side out; topstitch ½-inch hem.

To make ruffles, cut five print strips according to yardage estimate, above. Seam the ends to form rings. Topstitch ⅛-inch finished hem (see General Directions) on each raw edge. Gather each ruffle ½ inch down from the top edge to fit the under-skirt. Pin the ruffles on the skirt so the gathering thread on the top ruffle is ⅛ inch below the top seam, bottom ruffle barely touches the floor, and others are evenly spaced between. Ruffles should overlap. Topstitch on the gathering lines; remove pins.

Small Frame

MATERIALS
Fabric, print, ¼ yard
Heavyweight cardboard, 1 sheet
Foam, ¼-inch-wide, 5 × 7-inch piece
Lace, 1 yard ⅝-inch-wide
Ribbon, scrap ⅜-inch-wide
Artificial flowers
White glue
Mat knife

Cut two pieces of board, each 5 inches × 7 inches. Cut a centered 3 × 4-inch oval in one (front) cardboard. Glue foam to the front board and cut out an oval with mat knife. Cut two 7 × 9-inch pieces of fabric. Place front and back boards facedown on wrong side of the separate pieces of fabric. Wrap the fabric to wrong side and glue in place all around. Slash the fabric within the oval, wrap tabs to wrong side and glue. Glue lace around edges of the back piece so that it extends evenly beyond the piece. Place photograph on the back piece; add glue around edges near the lace; place front on back, with wrong sides together. Place a weight on the frame until dry.

Glue ribbon and flowers on front, following the photograph.

To make a stand, cut a 1½ × 6-inch piece of board. Cut fabric to fit both sides, then glue it on. Glue top 1 inch of the stand to back of the frame,

centering and aligning bottom of it with bottom of the frame. Bend the stand away from the frame.

Medium Frame

MATERIALS
Fabric, print, ½ yard
Foam, ¼-inch-thick, 8 × 10-inch piece
Heavyweight cardboard, 1 sheet
Lace, 1 yard each ⅜-inch-wide, ⅞-inch-wide
Ribbon, ½ yard ⅜-inch-wide
Artificial flowers
White glue
Mat knife

Follow directions for the small frame, cutting the cardboard 8 × 10 inches with 4¼ × 6½-inch oval cutout and cutting fabric 10 × 12 inches. Add the narrow lace edging to the wrong side of the front piece at the oval cutout and wider lace to the outer edges as for the small frame.

For a stand, follow directions for the small frame and cut a 1⅞ × 8¾-inch piece. Glue 1½ inches of it to the back of frame.

Large Mirror Frame

MATERIALS
Fabrics, 2 different prints, ½ yard each
Foam, ¼-inch-thick, 11 × 14-inch piece
Heavyweight cardboard, 2 sheets
Trim, 2 yards ½-inch-wide decorative edging
Ribbon, 6-inch scrap
Mirror, 8 × 10-inch
White glue
Mat knife

Follow directions for the small frame, working with a double thickness of cardboard throughout and cutting it to 11 × 14-inch outer dimensions with a 7½ × 9½-inch rectangular front cutout. Cut fabric 13 × 16 inches, using one print for the back and the other print for the front.

Glue mirror on the back. Use decorative edging in place of lace for the outer edge. For the inner edge, cut a ½ × 35-inch strip from the same fabric as back; fold it lengthwise and glue to the wrong side of front around the cutout area. Add decorative edging.

For a stand, follow directions for the small frame and cut two 3 × 13-inch pieces. Glue them together, then glue 2 inches of the stand to the back of the frame. Secure the bottom of the stand with a 6-inch scrap of ribbon, gluing ends of it to the frame bottom and the stand bottom.

MUSLIN READYMADES—YOUR WAY

I t's easy to perk up and personalize plain store-bought café curtains with lengths of ribbon (they could be patterned) that are topstitched to the muslin. Alternating ribbon stripes are topped by tacked-on bows.

MATERIALS
Café curtains, 1 pair unbleached muslin (each panel of ours is 42 inches wide × 25 inches long)
Grosgrain ribbon, for stripes, 10 yards, 1-inch-wide

Beginning and ending 1 inch from sides, mark each panel for five 1-inch-wide evenly spaced vertical ribbon stripes (ours are 8¾ inches apart.)

For the stripes, cut ten 23-inch lengths of ribbon (or the length from bottom of rod casing to lower edge plus ½ inch). Turn the ends under ¼ inch, then topstitch the side edges to the curtains.

Cut six 14-inch ribbons. Fold each to form a bow; pin to hold. Cut six 1¼-inch ribbons; fold ¼ inch to back on both sides of each; then tack the strip around the center of the bow. Tack a bow to the top of the first, third, and fifth stripe on each panel.

COZYING UP WITH ONE FABRIC

Studio bed, settee, wall covering, and shades are all done in one sheet pattern to warm and organize a typical guest-room's hodgepodge of furniture. For a special touch, the material is mitered on the couch pillows.

Studio Couch Cover

MATERIALS
Fabric or sheets, print and solid-color
   (see instructions to estimate yardage)
Cord, for welting, to fit around couch
   twice plus 6 times the mattress-to-
   floor measurement plus 5 yards for
   ties

Add ½ inch to all edges of the following pieces for seam allowance: Cut the cover top to the size of the mattress; cut the end panels and front and back panels the mattress-to-floor measurement and to fit the mattress size; cut two corner inserts 14 inches wide and mattress-to-floor deep; cut duplicate pieces from the lining fabric.

Make the welting ties first (see General Directions), cutting them into eight 22-inch lengths, then make the welting (see Corded Welting under General Directions).

With the raw edges matching, stitch the welting all around the right side of the cover top, around the sides and bottom of the front panel, around the bottom and front side edge of each end panel, and along the bottom of the corner inserts.

With right sides facing, stitch the end panels to the back panel. Repeat with the lining for ends and back.

With right sides facing and the welting sandwiched between, stitch the

linings to the matching print pieces, leaving an opening for turning. Turn the pieces right side out. With right sides facing, pin the corner inserts to the top in front, then pin front, end, and back panels to the top; stitch.

Sew the ties to corners as shown and tie into bows.

Couch Pillows

MATERIALS
Fabrics or sheets to match couch cover, ⅝ yard of print, 1 yard of solid color
Pillow forms, 20-inch, muslin-covered

Cut two 21-inch squares: a print front and a solid-color back. Cut four solid-color strips 2 × 21 inches for borders; on each, press one long edge under ½ inch. Pin, right side up, on the right side of the print square with raw edges matching; miter the corners (see General Directions). Topstitch the inner pressed edges. To assemble the cover, see Two-piece Pillow under General Directions.

Settee Cushion

MATERIALS
Fabric or sheet, print to match couch cover (see instructions to estimate yardage)

For the cushion, you will need one piece of fabric to cover the top and sides of the cushion and one piece to cover the bottom, adding ½-inch seam allowance to all edges. Cut out the two pieces.

Place the top piece, wrong side up,

on the cushion and pin the corners to fit. Stitch the corners and trim excess.

With right sides facing, stitch the top and bottom together, leaving the back open. Turn right side out, then insert the cushion and baste closed.

Settee Pillows

MATERIALS
Fabric or sheet, print to match couch cover, 1 yard
Pillow forms, 14-inch, muslin-covered

For each pillow, cut a 15-inch square front and back from floral fabric. See Two-piece Pillows under General Directions to complete the pillows.

Walls

MATERIALS
Fabric or sheets, print to match couch cover, enough to cover wall with sheet hems cut away or opened out and pressed

See Fabric-Covered Walls under General Directions. Remove any molding, and then replace or add it after the fabric has been applied to the walls.

Shades

MATERIALS
Fabric or sheet, print or solid-color to match couch cover
Do-it-yourself shade kit

To cover your shades with fabric, follow the instructions that come with the purchased shade kit.

PENNANT VALANCE WITH A NAUTICAL SNAP

Decorate a curtainless window with a heading of pennants flanked by longer banners—it couldn't be crisper. The heavy sailcloth valance is trimmed with craft supplier's wooden tassels painted to match.

MATERIALS

Fabric, heavy sailcloth or lightweight canvas (see instructions to estimate yardage)

Bias tape, 1-inch-wide, single-fold for appliqué

Flat wooden cutouts, 1 for each point (from crafts store)

Acrylic paint, to match fabric

Paintbrush

Double-faced carpet tape, valance width

Drill, curtain rod, rings (all optional)

Paper for pattern

Measure window area. Plan the center panel (ours is 18 inches long × about 98 inches wide), adding ½ inch all around for hem. To calculate the width of the points, divide the finished width measurement by the desired number of points (our valance has seven, each 14 inches wide).

To make a pattern, cut a strip of paper to one-point width; fold it in half lengthwise, then trim away the corners for a point pattern. Lightly pencil the pattern outline across one long edge of the center panel, allowing for hems at ends. Cut along the line. Cut two long banners the same width as the point, adding hem allowance; make a point on one end of each.

Turn ½-inch hem allowance under on all pieces, clipping at points; topstitch. Pin bias-tape appliqué to the front of the pointed edges of the banners and center panel, folding the tape to miter at top points (see General Directions); topstitch along edges of the tape.

If wooden cutouts have no holes, drill a small hole centered near the top. Paint the cutouts to match fabric. Sew them to the points.

Attach the center panel to the window frame and banners to the wall on each side with double-faced tape, or sew small rings to the valance and banner backs, then hang from rods.

GENERAL DIRECTIONS

STARTING UP

Enlarging Patterns

First, use a colored pencil and ruler to mark a grid on the pattern by connecting the grid lines around the edges.

An easy way to make a full-size pattern is to use graph paper (available at art stores) marked off into 1-inch squares. (If our pattern indicates that each square equals 2 inches, take a colored pencil and mark off the grid on your graph paper into 2-inch squares.)

On the graph paper, draw an outline around the same number of squares as there are on the pattern, taping sheets together, if necessary, to make a full-size pattern. In each square, draw the same pattern lines you see in the corresponding square on the pattern.

ESTIMATING YARDAGE

Estimating Yardage with String

This is a method of estimating yardage for a curtain swag or other form of draped valance. You will need a ball of string for measuring.

Simply drape the string around the window in the manner that pleases you, taping it to the window frame where necessary. The length of the string is the fabric yardage you will need to buy.

Visualizing Yardage Needs

Graph paper is also useful for visualizing the material you will need for a particular project. If you are using sheets, draw an outline to the scale of the sheet you are using, or draw a line representing the width of your yard goods. Then delineate the measurements of what you are making within those outlines.

Sheet Sizes

Twin: 66 × 96 inches; full: 81 × 96 inches; queen: 90 × 102 inches; king: 108 × 102 inches

Pattern for Slipcover

If you are replacing a worn slipcover, you can take it apart and use it as a pattern for the new slipcover.

FINISHING

Finished Hems

For a finished hem, fold the edge of your fabric twice and either topstitch or hand-sew on the wrong side. If, for instance, the instructions call for a ½-inch finished hem, fold and press the edge ½ inch to the wrong side, then fold and press it again another ½ inch.

BINDING AND WELTING

Bias Strips

Bias strips are mostly used to cover cord for welting or to bind an edge.

First, you must find the true crossgrain of the fabric. To do this, start close to one cut edge and pull out a thread the full width of the fabric, selvage to selvage. This will give you a narrow but visible line or channel; cut carefully along this line. Now, fold the fabric so that the cut edge (or crossgrain) meets the selvage on one side (see Diagram 1).

Cut along the diagonal fold; then, with a yardstick and soft pencil or

Diagram 1

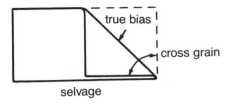

Diagram 2

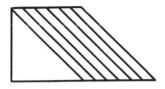

Diagram 3

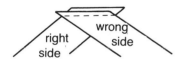

Corded Welting

Ready-made welting is available at sewing centers, but it may not be in the color you want. You can make welting with your own fabric by covering plain cable cord with bias strips.

Determine the width of the strip by folding a fabric scrap around the cord and marking it. Then, open the fabric flat and add ½-inch seam allowance outside each mark.

Cut your bias strips (see Bias Strips) and join them to measure the same length as your purchased cord. Fold the length *right* side out over the cord and stitch close to the cord with a zipper foot (see diagram).

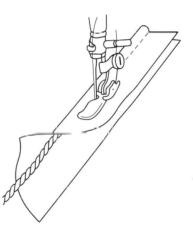

tailor's chalk, mark off strips of the desired width parallel to the diagonal edge (Diagram 2). Cut along the lines. Piece the strips by stitching them end to end to make the desired length (for instance, enough to cover a welting cord). To do this, stitch the diagonal ends together (½-inch seam allowance) as shown in Diagram 3. One yard of 45-inch-wide fabric will make a 2-inch-wide joined length of about 22 yards.

Welting Ties

Make the ties from uncut cord. Initially you will need cord double the total length of the ties. When the ties have been completed, however, this excess cord will be cut away to be used elsewhere, if necessary.

First, measure out to your *right* the total length of cord needed for all the ties; insert a pin marker at the determined length. Cut and piece a bias strip of fabric the same length (see Bias Strips). Fold the strip, *wrong* side out over the cord to the *left* of the marker; seam the strip close to the cord with a zipper foot and tack through the cord at the marker. Trim the seam allowance to about ⅛ inch. Starting at the marker, push the tube right side out over the cord to the *right* of the marker. When the measured section is enclosed, cut the cord at the marker, then cut the ties into equal lengths.

Push about ½ inch of the cord out one end of each tie and clip. Turn the ½ inch fabric inward and sew neatly. Sew the open end to the cover.

MITERED CORNERS

There is more than one way to miter a corner. To make one with a continuous strip of fabric, pin the strip, as specified, around the edge to be trimmed or along a marked square for appliqué. Each corner excess will stand up. If the *wrong* side of the strip is facing you (as for a binding that will be folded in half to the back), press the corner excess flat at a 45° angle, tacking it so it will hold its shape when the binding is folded over.

If the *right* side of the strip is facing you (as for an appliquéd trim), fold the corner excess inward at a 45° angle and press. When both edges of the strip are stitched, the corners will hold their shape, or you can topstitch or blind-stitch the diagonal folds.

To make a mitered corner with separate strips of fabric, simply cut all the strips with straight ends, then pin the strips around the piece to be trimmed, the ends overlapping at the corners. At each corner, fold the end of one strip diagonally over the straight end of the adjacent strip; stitch to secure.

PILLOWS

Two-piece Pillow
A two-piece pillow is a cover consisting of one piece for the front and one of identical size for the back.

Cut two identical pieces the size specified, or the size of the pillow form, adding ½-inch seam allowance all around. If you are adding welting or a ruffle, baste the welting first around the right side of the pillow front so that the raw edges of the welting and the pillow match. If there is a ruffle, pin it on top of the welting in the same manner, with raw edges matching. Then, with the right sides facing and the trim sandwiched between, stitch front and back together, leaving an opening on one side large enough to insert the pillow form.

Trim the seam allowance diagonally at the corners and turn the cover right side out. Insert the form, turn the seam allowance inside around the opening, and baste closed. You can, of course, insert a zipper if you prefer.

Three-piece Pillow
This pillow has one piece for the front and two for the back. The back pieces overlap at the center and form an opening through which you insert the pillow form.

Cut the pillow front and backs as specified. Or cut one piece the same size as the pillow form, adding ½-inch seam allowance all around, and then cut two backs. Cut two backs, each one half the size of the front plus 2 inches at the center edge for the overlapped opening. Topstitch ½-inch hem on the center edge of each back piece. With the hemmed edges overlapping, baste the back pieces together to form a piece the same size as the front.

Proceed in the same manner as for the Two-piece Pillow, adding any welting or ruffling, then stitching all four sides. Turn the cover right side out and insert the form. Add two or three snaps if desired.

CIRCULAR TABLECLOTH

To determine the size of the circle you will need, take the measurement from the floor, over the tabletop and down to the floor. This is the diameter of your finished cloth (you will need to add the specified amount for seam allowance). Most fabric is not wide enough for a floor-table-floor measurement without piecing (stitching pieces together to full size), so if you are using yard goods you will probably need to make your cloth in at least two pieces. A sheet, therefore, is the ideal fabric to use because it virtually eliminates piecing.

Determine the diameter of the full circle you will need, then cut a paper pattern one quarter the size, like a pie wedge.

Use a sheet or stitch lengths of fabric together that will form one piece large enough to accommodate the full circle needed. Fold the piece in half horizontally, then in half vertically. Pin your cut paper pattern to the fabric with the point at the folded corner; trace the curved edge of the pattern and cut out. Unfold the fabric into a full circle.

FABRIC-COVERED WALLS

Sheets are more practical to use as wall coverings than fabric by the yard because there will be fewer vertical seams than there would be with the narrower yard goods.

If there are floor or ceiling moldings, you can either remove them first and then replace them over the fabric edge, or you can leave the moldings in place and bring the fabric to them, then cover the fabric edge with trim.

With a helper, stretch a sheet along the top of the wall, stapling from the center edge to the corners. Pull the sheet taut and repeat the stapling process at the lower edge. Work in the same manner with each sheet, overlapping the vertical edges slightly and gluing them.

Either replace the moldings over the top and bottom stapled edges or cover the staples with a sheeting trim as follows: Cut 1½-inch-wide strips of sheet and press the long edges under ¼ inch. Glue the strips over the rows of staples at floor and ceiling.

BALLOON SHADES

Mark the position of the mounting board across the frame over the window and screw the angle irons into each end of the frame just below the board markings. Rest the board temporarily on the irons.

You will need a ball of string to determine the fabric width for the shade. Tape one end of the string at one end of the windowsill, then drape it across the sill, taping it into loops at equal distances apart (each loop represents a balloon section). The length of the string is the width of the fabric and the length of any ruffling you will need. You may have to piece the fabric to achieve the required width.

For the shade length, measure from the top edge of the window frame to the sill, adding 5 inches for the top hem. With the width and depth measurements, determine the fabric yardage or the number of sheets needed.

Cut out the shade, piecing it if necessary. Then, with yardstick and pencil, mark on the wrong side the width of each balloon section. Hem the sides. Add any ruffling required.

Turn the top edge under ½ inch, then 4 inches; baste. Cut the shirring tapes the length of the basted edge; stitch tape to the back of the hem 3 inches below the top edge.

Cut the ring tape into strips the length of the shade, aligning the rings. Cut one strip for each marked line separating the sections and one for each side edge.

Pin the tapes on the marked lines and side edges; topstitch both edges of each tape. Pull the strings on the shirring tape to gather the shade to the length of the mounting board. Knot and fasten the loose string ends on the wrong side.

With a helper, hold the shade against the board and mark on the bottom of the board the position of the ring tapes. Remove the shade and lift the board off the angle irons. For each tape, insert a screw eye in the bottom of the board. Screw the board permanently on the irons. Staple or tack the shirred edge of the shade to the board front.

Attach the pull-cord fastener to the side of the window frame. Tie the cord to the bottom ring on the tape at the *opposite* end of the window from the fastener; thread the cord up through the rings and across through all the screw eyes on the board; cut the cord 3 or 4 inches below the fastener. Starting with the bottom ring on the next tape, repeat the procedure for each tape (each cord will pass through one fewer screw eye; all will pass through the last screw eye).

Weight the shade by threading the metal rod through the bottom rings. To hold it in place, wrap thread tightly around the ends of the rod and sew to the tapes.

INDEX